KAPAP
COMBAT CONCEPTS

MARTIAL ARTS OF THE ISRAELI SPECIAL FORCES

By AVI NARDIA and ALBERT TIMEN
Special Adviser JOHN MACHADO

KAPAP
COMBAT CONCEPTS

MARTIAL ARTS OF THE ISRAELI SPECIAL FORCES

Edited by Sarah Dzida, Raymond Horwitz,
Jeannine Santiago and Jon Sattler

Graphic Design by John Bodine

Photography by Rick Hustead

©2008 Black Belt Communications LLC
All Rights Reserved
Printed in the United States of America
Library of Congress Control Number: 2007941887
ISBN-10: 0-89750-161-6
ISBN-13: 978-0-89750-161-3

First Printing 2008

WARNING

This book is presented only as a means of preserving a unique aspect of the heritage of the martial arts. Neither Ohara Publications nor the author makes any representation, warranty or guarantee that the techniques described or illustrated in this book will be safe or effective in any self-defense situation or otherwise. You may be injured if you apply or train in the techniques illustrated in this book and neither Ohara Publications nor the author is responsible for any such injury that may result. It is essential that you consult a physician regarding whether or not to attempt any technique described in this book. Specific self-defense responses illustrated in this book may not be justified in any particular situation in view of all of the circumstances or under applicable federal, state or local law. Neither Ohara Publications nor the author makes any representation or warranty regarding the legality or appropriateness of any technique mentioned in this book.

Kapap Academy LLC is a registered company in New Jersey. Albert Timen serves as its president and Avi Nardia acts as head instructor. For more information about the courses and training, please write to:

Kapap Academy LLC
P.O. Box 4027
River Edge, NJ 07661
USA

ACKNOWLEDGMENTS

Our deepest gratitude goes to all the contributors who made this project possible with their indispensable knowledge and assistance:

- John Machado for his friendship and guidance
- Lt. Col. (Res) Chaim Peer, who is the founder of the International Kapap Federation
- Dr. Yerucham Barak of Tel Aviv University
- David Arama of the International Kapap Federation in Israel
- Uri Kaffe, a *kapap* instructor
- *Hanshi* Patrick McCarthy for his support and instruction
- *Shihan* Jose Olivieri Rivera and Officer Robert Jobe of Shoshin Dojo for their years of help and friendship in keeping the "Way."
- Andre Zeitoun for his innovative contributions to kapap
- Guru Roger Agbulos, our brother and teacher for blades
- Jesse Abrescy and Ahmed Best for years of friendship and support
- Bram Frank of Common Sense Self-Defense Street Combat for his help and support
- Jaime Abregana Jr. from the Hawaiian Martial Arts International Society
- Dana L. Stamos for her support in our cause and for her long-term friendship
- Officer Tad Nelson and Scott Seroll—our kapap instructors—for their help in editing and photographing the book, as well as their years of support
- Brian Hepp for believing in us and the "kapap way"
- Dr. Eldad Haruvi for his assistance with historical research and photos
- Noah Gross from Israel for his contributions and help with kapap history
- Alfredo Tucci for all his years of help
- Jim Wagner, who was the first person outside of Israel to recognize kapap as a reality-based fighting system
- Fred Host for all his help throughout the years with stunt, tactical, Brazilian *jiu-jitsu* and ground training
- Robert W. Young and the *Black Belt* crew for all their years of support
- Our wonderful families for their support and encouragement
- Yelena Savranskaya, Ira S. Lifland, Andres Sepulveda, Eric Simpson, Officer Frank Bordonaro, Sam A. Markey, Craig and Deborah Welsh, Martin Nielson, Tanner Nystrom, Nathan and his father Joseph John, Josh Maiman, Joe Fachler, the Shoshin Dojo students, Mary Mendez Rizzo, Rose Mary Mahoney, Armando Olivieri Rivera, Len Boucher, Matt Kilgore, Paul Colon, Mario Caletz and Joseph McGee

DEDICATION

This book is dedicated to the original instructors of *kapap*: Maishel Horovitz, Gerson Kopler, Yehuda Marcus, Avraham Zakai, Yitzchak Stibel and Moshe Finkel.

FOREWORD

On February 23, 2000, I received an invitation from Maj. Avi Nardia to come to Israel and teach the country's top police and military defensive-tactics instructors my Knife Survival course, which is part of my Reality-Based Personal Protection system. A few months later, I found myself at the Israeli Police Operational Fitness Academy in Havatselet Hasharon teaching a room full of professionals and feeling honored that warriors I respected would integrate my methods into their own tactics.

After fulfilling my teaching obligations, Avi asked whether there was anything he could do for me in return. I had an immediate answer for him. I said, "Yes, I want to learn your current shooting techniques. Plus, I'd like to learn Israeli hand-to-hand combat." An hour later, I was at a firing range with my instructor, Sgt. Uri Kaffe, to practice shooting techniques with Uzi submachine guns, Galil rifles, BUL pistols and hundreds of rounds of ammunition. After the smoke cleared on my practice session, however, Avi introduced me to the original Israeli martial art of *kapap*.

Like anyone who has trained with Avi, I was impressed with his abilities and toughness. Although a small man in stature, he is one of the deadliest fighters I have ever met. Of course, his personal history reflects his warrior spirit: He was a member of the counterterrorist team YAMAM, an acronym for *Yehidat Mishtara Meyuhedet*, which is a special unit of the Israeli Border Patrol. At the time I first met Avi, however, he was the lead defensive-tactics instructor for the national police academy as well as an officer for the Israeli Army Reserve.

When I returned to the United States, I invited Avi to come teach his techniques to police and military units in California, and he accepted the offer. Once stateside, he freely shared his expertise on Israeli tactics, suicide bombers and kapap to the participants of that first seminar in 2001, which included the FBI, the Los Angeles County Sheriff's Department, the Orange County SWAT team, the U.S. Marines from Camp Pendleton and various other local agencies. As expected, Avi was a big hit, so I flew him out to the United States a couple more times to teach seminars in other states. As such, interest in kapap started to grow within the professional community.

My second training trip to Israel was even better than the first because Avi took me around and introduced me to the who's who of the Israeli security forces and military martial arts community, including Lt. Col. Chaim Peer (now in the Israeli Reserves), a well-respected war hero and the chief kapap instructor at the time. We also visited important historical locations, like the cave where the Palmach practiced during World War II. At the same time, however, as Avi and I were going between each other's countries, the civilian martial arts community remained familiar only with *Krav Maga*, an Israeli martial art codified and modified by Imi Lichtenfeld in the 1970s.

That all changed in 2003 when I wrote an article for *Black Belt* about the Israeli martial arts I had personally trained in, namely Krav Maga, *hisardut*, *lotar* and kapap. Readers were surprised to learn that Krav Maga was not the only Israeli martial art, and they heard Avi Nardia's name for the first time. Little did I know that the article would create an even bigger civilian appetite for the Israeli martial arts, especially kapap.

After the article came out, I called Avi and told him that he should consider developing a civilian version of kapap, which he should teach in the United States and Europe. He told me, "That's an interesting idea. I'll think about it." A couple of weeks later, Avi said that he was not interested because he was too involved with his current police and military obligations.

By the end of 2003, Avi had invited me to Israel again to train at the famous Wingate Institute Bahad 8 military base. I was one of the few foreign instructors to ever train troops there, and I also had the opportunity to help Avi during a Special Forces selection process. While we watched young soldiers run an obstacle course, I told Avi once again that he should reconsider my advice because the American market was ripe for kapap, but Avi still declined.

Two months after my visit, Avi called me and said, "Jim, I think you're right. I think that there should be a civilian version of kapap, and I need your help." Within a few months, Avi had taken a sabbatical from his police job in Israel, rented out his house in Netanya, and moved to Los Angeles with his family. In fact, he started teaching kapap almost as soon as the plane touched down at Los Angeles International Airport.

Because Avi had charisma and because kapap was an effective reality-based system, it wasn't long before kapap started to spread internationally. Throughout the process, Avi has sought my advice, and in turn, I have taken advantage of his tutelage. When I officially formed the Reality-Based Personal Protection system for civilians back in January 2003, I incorporated many techniques that I had learned from Avi. Also, when I now travel around the world to teach, I always mention my friend and his contributions to my system.

In this book, you will find authentic kapap tactics and techniques from a seasoned Israeli warrior who not only is one of the top police officers in the Israeli Defense Force but also is the man who brought the obscure martial art of kapap into the limelight. With these techniques and training methods, your own martial arts skills will progress. Or as they say in the Israeli military—*kadeema!* Forward!

Jim Wagner
Founder, Reality-Based Personal Protection
Black Belt Hall of Fame member (2006 Self-Defense Instructor of the Year)

TABLE OF CONTENTS

Acknowledgments 5

Dedication 6

Foreword 7

Chapter 1: Introduction 10

Chapter 2: Origin and Evolution 15

Chapter 3: Basic Principles 20

Chapter 4: Relative Position 28

Chapter 5: Conditioning 64

Chapter 6: The Art of Impact 90

Chapter 7: Liability in the Modern World 116

About the Kapap Academy 118

About the Authors 119

About the Advisers 120

CHAPTER 1: INTRODUCTION

What is *kapap*?

Simply put, KAPAP is an acronym for the generic Hebrew phrase *Krav Panim El Panim*, which literally translates to "face-to-face combat" and can be applied to any combat style, martial art or physical confrontation. This means that regardless of whether the opponents are soldiers in a standoff or judo wrestlers in a competition, they are kapap fighters. In more complex terms, however, kapap is a dynamic self-defense system that continues to emphasize the abilities and experience of the individual over techniques.

It's also correct to say that unlike traditional fighting styles, modern kapap is neither a competitive sport nor a martial art. Instead, it is a combat doctrine that helps the individual prepare for life-or-death situations by combining various fighting styles to create that person's most effective defense. Typically, traditional martial arts and fighting systems have unintentional built-in barriers that restrict their practitioners with rules and regulations that have been around for centuries. For example, some traditional styles only teach one approach to combat or only pass on the teachings of a single person. These systems and techniques may still have modern value, but often they are too static because instructors teach by rote or students only learn techniques in a sterile environment, like a gym.

Take, for instance, a traditional martial artist who is attacked at night. In the contained world of his training center, he usually only faces opponents who know how to attack with his style's specific techniques. However, in the real world, the martial artist faces an unpredictable and potentially dangerous situation because his attacker may ambush him with techniques from another system. Of course, there is a chance that the martial artist's traditional style will prove more than adequate for dealing with a random attacker, but there is a greater chance that he will have to improvise his way out of the fight. Stuck in the structure of his established martial art, he may have never learned how to take his techniques to the street and question their relevance in the modern world.

To properly prepare for combat, training must be varied and realistic. Kapap practitioners train both indoors and outdoors, in the water and on solid surfaces, in poorly lit areas and while blinded by flashlights to accustom themselves to the stress of a real attack. This is why kapap, as taught by the Kapap Academy, is one of the most successful modern combat and mixed-martial arts systems out there because it blends the best of traditional martial arts with modern applications for practical self-defense. Rather than focusing on techniques, belts or levels, kapap instructors create a fluid reality-based training program for students based on their individual expectations and abilities. From the very beginning, instructors encourage their students to ask questions and make suggestions for new techniques or counters. This also helps students understand that every question or problem has a logical answer and that the solution for one person may not apply to another.

For example, it doesn't make sense for an instructor to teach a 120-pound woman how to perform a judo throw on a 250-pound man because she is physically incapable of performing the technique against him. This is not an insult to the woman's physical ability; rather, her instructor recognizes that a person with a smaller frame has different advantages and disadvantages against a larger opponent. While the woman should still learn the judo technique because it could be used against her, the instructor must be creative, inquisitive and think like a kapap fighter to properly prepare her to deal with the threat. In order to make her effective against her attacker, the instructor must ask, What techniques will work best for a slight woman in a real fight?

This is the key to kapap: Use only what works for you. By exploring your own strengths and weaknesses, you can build a customized "toolbox" of techniques that will prove effective in any random conflict. Remember, kapap is not a magical solution to becoming a better martial artist, and it is not going to immediately increase your strength or fighting ability. Instead, kapap is about gradually upgrading your "toolbox" with physical skills, practical exercises, effective techniques and common sense through a variety of resources. Kapap is also one of the few combat systems in which the student and the teacher experience parallel roles. As the student expands his knowledge based on his own pace and expectations, the kapap instructor does, too. Despite possessing a vast amount of experience from their past law-enforcement and military careers, kapap instructors must also continue to branch out and explore new perspectives of combat to keep up with the ever-changing threats that their students face.

That's why it's important to understand that this book is not intended to replace your daily training routine. Instead, the purpose of this book is to serve as a reference for kapap's basic forms and principles to help kapap students and instructors, as well as beginners and established martial artists, understand its origins. Take a moment to see which of the following categories applies to you.

For people with no martial arts background ...

As someone without any martial arts experience, you can start at the beginning. Rather than learn self-defense from rules, regulations or doctrines, try to shape your martial arts training with techniques that work best for you. However, don't be fooled into thinking that this book will be a shortcut to combat success. While it will give you a good idea on where to start your studies on practical self-defense, you should invest time in exploring your combat options through traditional or mixed martial arts. An instructor, whether kapap or otherwise, can also help you take the principles in this book and use them to gradually improve your skill level.

Additionally, understanding the different forms, history and evolution of a sport or combat system will help you identify its key components, which can be universally effective in a real fight. Because practical self-defense is based on the knowledge and experience of reality-based and traditional skills that have been refined through the years, this book will teach beginners how to integrate those skills with kapap's essential principle: Use what's best for you.

For people who already practice kapap ...

For those who understand kapap, this book will serve as a practical reminder of the basic practices, principles, drills and techniques of the instructors at the Kapap Academy. These include:

- relative position
- balance displacement
- the principle of two points of contact
- the push-pull principle
- how to manipulate the upper and lower body into T-shapes
- the "Frankenstein"
- the "Elvis"
- geometric elements in attacks and defenses
- the pre- and post-conflict aspects of a fight
- mandatory CPR training
- kapap triangles, which are systems composed of three principles

Take the techniques and concepts that you read in this book and analyze them with your students or instructor in order to master them. However, students should remember that this book should not replace training with a qualified kapap instructor.

For practitioners of other martial arts or combat systems ...

Rather than look for contradictions between your martial art and kapap, consider how the many ideas and techniques in this book complement it. Even if you know many of the techniques in this book, examining them through the lens of kapap's principles will give you a new understanding of how they work and will help steer your training in a new direction.

This book will also introduce many martial artists to "relative position," which deals with the spatial relationship between two opponents and their environment. This may seem like a simple concept, but it is actually a vital combat principle that is rarely explored in many self-defense systems. The book's detailed analysis of it will help martial artists complement their training by increasing their operational awareness.

****

Regardless of your skill level, this book will show you how to launch an effective attack or defense in a face-to-face combat situation. Remember, kapap is not about grandmasters, belts, ranks or egos. It is about learning safety and maintaining the best trophy or belt of them all—your life!

Chapter 1

◄ A kapap student practices shooting with only one hand while on the back of a motorcycle. This forces the student to find his balance before he engages the target.

Photos courtesy of Avi Nardia

► Students simulate an airplane or bus hostage situation while one student pretends to be a terrorist. The students use their decision-making skills, as well as their determination, to disarm the dangerous opponent.

◄ Using a rubber knife, two students attack each other at a realistic speed. The instructor observes any deadly hits or mistakes the students make, which he will review with them, while their fellow classmates observe and learn from the fight. For safety, the two sparring students wear goggles and protective gear.

► At the Kapap Boot Camp in California, students increase their physical stamina by training on the beach, where they are exposed to natural elements as well as different surfaces.

KAPAP: Combat Concepts

◄ In order to keep their balance during stressful conditions, kapap students practice resistance training at various water levels.

► Close-quarters combat training is about fighting in confined spaces, such as buildings, elevators, stairways, cars, parking garages, buses and airplanes. Here, a young woman cross-trains on a stairway to see how much power her kick needs to floor her opponent.

◄ In order to deal with post-conflict consequences, students learn how to administer CPR on both adult and child dummies.

CHAPTER 2: ORIGIN AND EVOLUTION

Born out of necessity, kapap started out as a method of self-defense created by Jewish settlers in Palestine and was originally used to describe the rudimentary tactics of those farmers and shepherds during the first half of the 20th century. Because times have changed, however, and so have the dangers that modern people face, the kapap practiced today by the Kapap Academy is far different from the face-to-face combat used by its original creators. Whereas the early practitioners only needed kapap to protect their homes from local violence, today's world faces a diversity of potential dangers. That's why kapap was and continues to be based on necessity. Even though it has switched hands from shepherds to soldiers and from soldiers to civilians, kapap has maintained its trademark adaptability and flexibility even after 50 years.

The Historical Period: 1920s to 1970s

In the years following World War I, the League of Nations authorized the British Mandate of Palestine, which allowed Jewish immigrants to reconstitute the nation of Israel. In the early 1920s and '30s, small groups of mostly European Jews took advantage of this open policy to settle in remote locations among Palestine's predominantly Arab population. During this period, the British governed Palestine, but they were more concerned with its importance as a strategic transportation route than with potential internal friction among ethnic groups. In addition to this, the local Arab population was mainly made up of rural villagers who were unaccustomed to the more urban and European developments of the Jewish settlements. Moreover, local Arab leaders and clergy stirred up anti-Semitic feelings among the population, which led people to steal from and vandalize Jewish homesteads.

Thus the Hashomer, Israel's first defense organization, was formed. It was a loosely organized security detail that patrolled the Jewish settlements and defended them against attacks. The Hashomer also used the very first form of kapap, which was a scattered method of defense that relied heavily on what was at hand, like shovels, sticks or tools—basically anything that was available to a shepherd or farmer.

Between 1936 and 1939, Palestine experienced its largest wave of Jewish immigration as well as witnessed its largest attacks against Jewish settlements. Whatever the reason for the increased violence, the British finally stepped in to appease the growing resentment of the Arab majority. In order to maintain their control over the area, the British government denied European-Jewish refugees entry into Palestine. They also forbade Jewish settlers from carrying or training with firearms under penalty of death unless they were recognized members of the Hashomer.

Despite massive waves of legal and illegal immigrants, Jews still only made up 10 percent to 15 percent of the entire population of Palestine. With their limited means of defense, the Jewish settlements, known collectively as the *yishuv*, came together and pulled their defensive resources on a national scale. Thus, the Haganah was formed. Created in 1920, it didn't become a truly operational or substantive force until 1929 during one of the largest riots against the yishuv. From this point on, however, specific dates are difficult to document because the

Haganah, with whom the Hashomer would eventually merge, was an underground movement that operated on two levels: legal and illegal. Through legal means, the Jewish settlements worked with the British to form special night squads commanded by a British officer, Orde Charles Wingate. By supervising the Haganah's nightly patrols, the British hoped to balance out and also extricate themselves from regional tensions. Through illegal means unknown to the British, however, the Haganah trained secretly in arms and various forms of face-to-face combat, which they called "kapap."

Around 1939, kapap truly started to take shape through the Haganah, who changed it from a passive form of self-defense into an active combat doctrine. Instead of using kapap solely for defense, the Haganah employed it as an offensive tool against their Arab neighbors. This meant that the yishuv began to actively fight back.

In addition to this, the Haganah only recruited immigrants who could add to the unit's combative assets, which helped supplement kapap with a number of new offensive and defensive techniques. In fact, this variety is no more apparent than in the Haganah members who were also the original kapap instructors:

- Gershon Kopler was a judo and *jujutsu* instructor who incorporated his techniques into kapap's self-defense concepts.
- Yehuda Marcus, also a judo and jujutsu teacher, was the chief kapap instructor for the Haganah and their operational division known as the Palmach.
- Moshe Finkel was a combat-conditioning instructor who contributed fitness applications, which included long-distance running and walking with a heavy load, tug of war, obstacle courses and rock climbing.
- Yitzchak Stibel was the head boxing instructor for the Palmach, and his techniques are still used for speed, stamina and mobility training.
- Maishel Horovitz, kapap's head instructor, helped develop short-stick fighting (which was prevalent in kapap's earlier years) into something more versatile.

Today, many modern kapap concepts emulate the same ideas that were used by the original instructors to teach their troops. The only difference is that they have been upgraded to fit a modern era with modern issues.

While the stick was the most available weapon to the yishuv, the massive influx of knowledge from new immigrants meant that the Haganah had many different combat styles to improvise with and combine. In addition to this, the Haganah reached out beyond Palestine and offered protection to Jewish communities in places like Lebanon, Syria and Algeria by teaching them their face-to-face fighting techniques. From these experiences, Haganah members would return with new combat knowledge to add to kapap. As the years progressed, the system eventually was united into one doctrine and included an instructor program, which ensured that each official kapap teacher would have access to the same diverse pool of knowledge, experience and training.

But times changed and so did kapap. In 1948, Israel declared its independence from Britain and was attacked. With the conventional armies of Egypt, Syria, Jordan, Lebanon and Iraq as its opponents, Israel did not need a militia like the Haganah but a legitimate military force to cope with tanks, foot soldiers and modern weaponry. Because of this, the Haganah renamed itself the Israeli Defense Force and became the official national army of Israel practically overnight. IDF soldiers no longer needed to know guerrilla or close-quarters combat tactics as much as before, and kapap became a secondary weapon before it soon became the exclusive domain of the Israeli Special Forces.

At this point in history, the word "kapap" begins to disappear from use because it is replaced by terms more suited to the form of combat being practiced by the Israeli Special Forces. This came about because of the rise of the legendary Unit 101, a special-forces unit Ariel Sharon led in 1954. During its six to eight months of existence, the group paved a new road for special operations, which meant that the term Krav Panim El Panim, or face-to-face combat, just didn't fit anymore. *Lochama zeira* became the new term, which literally translates to "special-operations combat," and would remain in use until the 1970s. While it still encompassed kapap techniques, one of lochama zeira's main distinctions was that each special-forces operator trained to act individually and not as a unit. In fact, this new style was so successful that the IDF central command opened a special warfare school where students had to pass a mandatory qualification course known as the *Maslul* to become a special operator. This test would also be necessary for *lotar* operators, which consequently became the next step in kapap's evolution.

With the rise of modern terrorism in the 1970s, kapap changed once again to fit the needs of the time. To deal with events like plane hijackings and bombings, Israel created lotar, the country's first school of thought regarding terrorism. LOTAR is an acronym for *Lohama Neged Teror*, which means "counter-terror combat." The training doctrines of the new school were divided into three main directives: The IDF counterterrorism school operated under the military, the Israeli Security Service (or the SHABAK) operated under the government, and the BATAP (or civilian police) operated under the chief of staff and the Home Affairs Office minister. These divisions of lotar remained in Israel, where they had to be conscious of their actions because they could affect innocent bystanders. Surrounded by a friendly civilian population, operators of lotar divisions patrolled along the same routes and settlements that the Hashomer once guarded more than half a century earlier.

Modern Period: 1980s to Present

With the rise of Israel's new counterterrorist unit, the word "lotar" came to stand for military kapap and still does today. This means that between the 1970s and the 1990s, the word "kapap" almost disappeared from use. If it was mentioned, people usually associated it with its historical origins or as a variation of *Krav Maga*, a better-known Israeli martial art. Despite its disappearance from the public, however, kapap still remained an important part of the training and lives of the men and women in the Israeli military, especially the officers of the Israeli Special Forces, like Lt. Col. Chaim Peer and Maj. Avi Nardia, who both now serve in the Reserves.

In 2000, these two officers decided to preserve not only the original term "kapap" but also the principle that combat is based on necessity. To do this, they created the International Kapap Federation and began to bring kapap back into the mainstream culture. With a few other kapap instructors from their time in the IDF, the two men began to distinguish modern kapap from its older versions. These distinctions are:

- It is the first form of kapap to be taught outside of Israel.
- It is now taught to civilians, which no longer makes it an exclusive military combat system.

Eventually, Nardia formed the Kapap Academy with several other Israeli kapap and lotar instructors, like Albert Timen, to legitimize this fluid self-defense and combat system through a flexible but established structure.

****

As you can see, kapap has changed and evolved over the years. It has been used by settlers, militiamen, soldiers and civilians as a form of self-defense and shaped by the experiences of its practitioners. In fact, the modern kapap that is taught by the Kapap Academy bases most of its teachings on the real-life experience of its military and law-enforcement instructors, which now include personnel from outside of the IDF. Recognizing their system's adaptable nature, the instructors rely on their past experiences but also look ahead and are open to learning new techniques and tactics. This is why Brazilian *jiu-jitsu* will be mentioned often in the book. Because Nardia is always looking to upgrade his toolbox, he reached out to his friend, jiu-jitsu champion and teacher John Machado, to help him incorporate jiu-jitsu tactics into kapap's principles.

Also, modern kapap is more than just a combat doctrine used by the military. Because it is taught to civilians and defense groups outside of Israel, kapap instructors must be aware that the legality of certain defenses or attacks may change from culture to culture or country to country. They have to spend more time developing practical skills that can be adapted by people of any age, gender, strength or skill level. This is why even from its humble beginnings as a marginalized and underground art, kapap has become one of the most effective and successful mixed martial arts of the modern era.

◄ Avi Nardia's father, Josef Nardia, teaches kapap to the first Israeli Special Forces unit in 1950. Dressed in full gear, his students perform techniques under stress at an obstacle course. (Because he is the directing drill sergeant, Josef Nardia is not shown in this picture.)

Photos courtesy of Avi Nardia

► Josef Nardia (far left) with his platoon while they practice a weapon-shooting stance.

◄ Josef Nardia (far right) teaches kapap knife-fighting skills. From how the fighters hold their weapons and position their bodies, it's obvious that these knife tactics were borrowed from fencing principles.

CHAPTER 3: BASIC PRINCIPLES

Kapap is a combat system based on principles rather than techniques because all close-quarters combat styles are governed by similar ideas. When you truly know and understand these ideas, then you'll be able to break down any technique—regardless of its origin or style. This is why kapap fighters are known for being versatile opponents; they usually seem able to handle themselves against many kinds of attacks. In this chapter, we'll discuss the basic principles that influence how kapap practitioners usually train and fight.

The Kapap Triangle

The "kapap triangle" shows students how to train and become balanced fighters by helping them remember and understand basic principles of face-to-face combat. The number "three" or the "idea of three" is common in kapap philosophies. For example, there is a triangle to describe the three types of people in a conflict: the "yes" person, who always does what he is told; the "no" person, who never does what he is told; and the "maybe" person, whose actions are the most difficult to predict because he can change his mind at any given time.

The most important triangle, however, is the kapap triangle, which embodies the Kapap Academy's main training philosophy and consists of three elements:

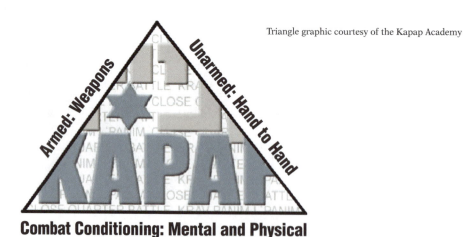

Triangle graphic courtesy of the Kapap Academy

As the base of the triangle, combat conditioning is the foundation for the other two concepts. A kapap fighter's armed and unarmed combat ability is affected by his mind-set, which is developed through mental and physical conditioning. Often, people believe they will win a fight if they look "mean" or "tough," but it doesn't work that way in real life. Being too confident can be a double-edged sword because, while it can intimidate your opponent, it may also cause them to overestimate your abilities and attack more ferociously. As a result, your opponent may attack you with a force you are neither mentally nor physically prepared to face.

Kapap students use combat conditioning to strengthen their "toolbox" of skills, which is why it's the foundation of the kapap triangle. Learning how to manage stress, identify and face natural fears, and overcome paralyzing mental stoppages will increase your effectiveness in combat, speed up your reaction time and make you more self-reliant.

As a leg of the kapap triangle, unarmed combat is a set of practical skills. By exploring other martial arts and combat systems through training with a kapap instructor, you can filter out the techniques that will not help you dominate an unarmed conflict.

In contrast, armed combat is the side of the kapap triangle that focuses on understanding and becoming proficient in modern weaponry. Practitioners learn how to improvise and make any tool a weapon, preparing them for situations in which conventional weapons may not be available. Along with principles from the kapap weapon triangle, this leg of the triangle includes training in small firearms and bladed weapons.

Using the kapap triangle will help you invest your time equally among all three categories and recognize your weaknesses, which will identify practices and techniques to study next. For instance, if you train exclusively for hand-to-hand combat competitions, you may lack the combat conditioning necessary for a real conflict and be unable to perform the techniques under extreme pressure. With the help of kapap instructors, students train to increase their mental and physical endurance. While independent study can help you balance your combat readiness in many ways, training with a certified Kapap Academy instructor will usually give you more satisfying results.

The Kapap Weapon Triangle

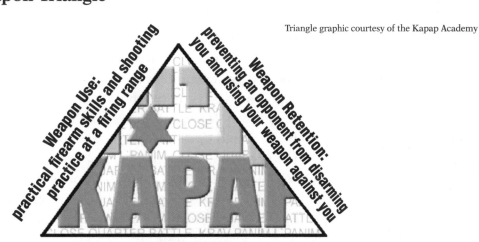

Triangle graphic courtesy of the Kapap Academy

Unlike the kapap triangle, the principles of this triangle are intertwined and of equal importance. For example, a student learns the following during a gun drill of any kind:

- how to take his adversary's weapon away
- how certain tactics help his opponent retain the gun
- how to keep the weapon from being used against him
- how to operate the weapon once he disarms his opponent

The same idea is true for knife retention, disarms and use. When you practice one aspect of this triangle, you practice all three.

Relative Position

This kapap principle outlines how a fighter should position himself relative to his opponent(s) and the environment during a fight. It is covered in greater depth in the next chapter.

Movement

"Economy of motion" is the main concept behind movement in kapap. In order to achieve it, conserve your energy in a fight by using small moves rather than impressive or flamboyant ones, and maintain the flow and energy of your movements through logical combinations. Basically, if you launch a punch and it misses, you probably shouldn't try to draw your weapon or hit your opponent with another punch. If you did, you would have to finish the motion of the failed punch, get into a new position and then fire or strike at your opponent again. Instead, an elbow strike would be a more logical and economical attack because it maintains the motion of the first failed punch while closing the distance between you and your target.

In order to confuse and disorient your opponent through movement, your footwork and attacks should be as unpredictable as the whirling of a gyroscope, which is why kapap instructors refer to this principle as the "gyro." If your last attack was thrown at his head, attack his body. If your opponent expects you to move right, cut left. Another common gyro is the high-low-high triangle, which can be seen in the sequence above (1); the defender confuses his opponent by hitting a high target, like the face (2), then a low target, like the groin (3), and then a high target (4). By keeping your opponent off-balance, he won't be able to put any weight behind his attacks.

Manipulation Through T-Shapes

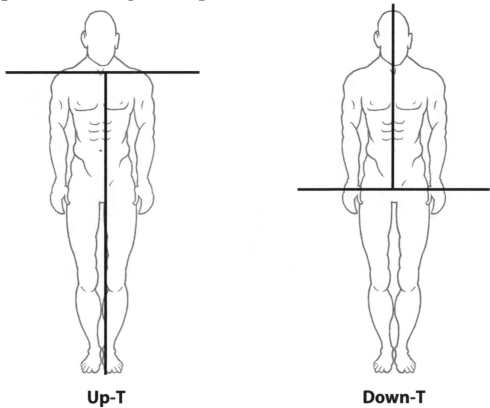

Up-T   **Down-T**

T-shapes are areas of the body that maintain balance, which kapap practitioners manipulate in order to unbalance their opponents. The up-T is the traceable T-shape of the body's vertical centerline combined with the horizontal line made by the shoulders. In contrast, the down-T refers to the T-shape made by the body's vertical centerline combined with the horizontal line made by the hips.

Because the T-shapes outline the body's balance centers, controlling them can decide the entire conflict's course. For example, if a kapap practitioner pushes a particular point on a T-shape, he can knock his opponent down. Or if the kapap practitioner pins his opponent's left shoulder down to the ground, which is the left part of the up-T, he neutralizes the person's entire left side. Basically, his opponent can be knocked off-balance or immobilized because of one hit on a T.

Reading an opponent's T-shapes is also important because doing so will give you more time to block or launch an attack. For instance, a boxer will usually look at his opponent's chest—which is part of the horizontal line of the up-T—instead of his eyes. He does this because he doesn't want to telegraph his next move or get faked out by a misleading glance from his opponent. The chest, however, never lies because all strikes start from there. Basically, a boxer can tell whether an opponent will hit with the right hand because his chest shifts to the right. Likewise, because all kicks are launched from the hips, watching the down-T will give you a better read on what your opponent might do next.

The Push-Pull Principle

Knocking your opponent off-balance is common in any martial art, and the push-pull principle is important to remember in a fight—especially when you have to improvise. By choosing two points to manipulate, such as on his T-shapes, you can unbalance any opponent. After choosing which targets to manipulate, pull one point while pushing the other, forcing the two away from each other. For example, as illustrated by the pictures, pushing a person's right shoulder while pulling his right leg will force him in two different directions (1).

It's also not necessary to limit your targets to points on the T-shapes. For instance, two opponents might grapple, with one on top and the other on the bottom. The opponent on the bottom pulls at his attacker's face and pushes at his shoulder (3). This forces the attacker to roll off him or risk having his neck broken. You can also mix points with points on the T-shapes. A kapap practitioner can just as easily unbalance and control an opponent by pulling at his head and pushing at his shoulder (2). As you can see, this principle can be useful in any conflict, but a fighter must be creative and quick-witted to use it to his advantage.

The Principle of Two Points of Contact

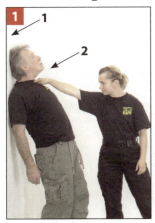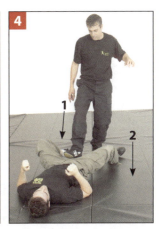

In most hand-to-hand conflicts, a fighter maintains contact with two points in order to manipulate a certain body part. For instance, most arm locks require your hands to be placed on different locations of an opponent's arm—like the wrist, elbow or shoulder—to control his movements. What differentiates this concept from the push-pull principle is that it can apply to any two points, whether on or off the body. You can either manipulate two points on the opponent's body (2, 3) or one point on his body and another on a surface (1, 4).

Balance Displacement

Like the push-pull principle or manipulation of the T-shapes, this concept focuses on unbalancing your opponent. The main difference is that balance displacement can apply to many techniques like choke holds (1), slips (2) or arm and leg sweeps (3, 4). It can also simply refer to a bad step backward because sometimes you don't need to make contact with your opponent to cause a misstep.

For example, an attacker throws a punch at a martial artist. The martial artist avoids the hit, which makes the attacker overextend. Without touching him, the martial artist gains an advantage in the fight by causing the opponent to lose his balance. The opponent must now recover his balance before he can launch an attack, whereas the martial artist is free to attack, defend or escape—it's his choice and his game.

Geometric Elements in Attacks and Defenses

Every martial art and combat system is based on geometric attacks or defenses. There are linear techniques (2, 4), such as arm strikes like uppercuts or straight kicks to the front, side or back. There are circular techniques (1, 3), such as arm strikes like hooks or roundhouse kicks. There are also triangular techniques like choke holds (5). In the end, any technique, no matter where it was created, can be broken down into the same simple forms and principles. No matter who the kapap practitioner's enemy is, the practitioner can use this knowledge to analyze and create an effective defense against any attack.

The Pre- and Post-Conflict Aspects of a Fight

Most martial artists agree that the best way to fight is to avoid one altogether. If calling the police is your best option against five opponents, call the police. Kapap takes this concept a step further by breaking it down into pre- and post-conflict situations.

"Pre-conflict" refers to anything and everything you can do not only to avoid a fight but also to prepare for it. This includes, among other things, stress conditioning, mental and physical endurance exercises, and traditional training.

"Post-conflict" refers to anything and everything you can do to avoid the consequences after a fight, such as injuries or legal actions. This includes first aid, learning what constitutes proper force in certain situations, etc. For example, a rapist puts a knife to a woman's throat in a parking lot and tells her to get in her car with him. Fortunately, the woman has been trained to look ahead and consider her post-conflict options. She realizes that her chances of rescue and remaining safe are better if she defends herself in the parking lot rather than wherever the rapist plans on taking her, so she takes action immediately. Even if the woman is injured during the conflict, she still made the right decision because she gauged the consequences and acted accordingly.

Mandatory CPR Training

Kapap practitioners build themselves a "toolbox" of methods to prepare themselves for any situation. In order to do that, they learn CPR and first aid because even basic medical training can help save their life. Knowing how to properly make and tie a tourniquet can prevent massive bleeding if someone gets cut during a fight. From heart attacks to knife wounds, medical training will help you handle the post-conflict aspects of a fight. For example, it's a bad idea to remove the blade from a knife wound because it might cut a new vessel when taken out. Or if someone isn't breathing, you may need to perform CPR or direct others to help you.

****

In the end, kapap does not teach its practitioners to rely solely on techniques. Instead, they must understand the universal principles behind techniques so they can counter any move that's thrown at them, even if it's from another system.

CHAPTER 4: RELATIVE POSITION

Imagine this: At the outset of a fight, you make a move that not only gives you a positional advantage over your opponent but also helps you control him for the rest of the conflict. Such an idea may sound too good to be true or even too complex to learn, but it's not. You will increase your chances of success by calculating your relative position.

So what is relative position? Simply put, it is the best position for you to be in at any particular moment and is determined by your environment and the position of your opponents. By taking your situation, condition, state, position, stance and posture into account, you'll be able to maintain the advantage throughout a fight.

Here's an example: A highly trained police officer encounters a suspect on the street at night. As the officer approaches the suspect, he immediately analyzes his first relative position as compared to that of the suspect. He quickly considers questions like the following:

- Where's the best place to **situate** my body in this location so I have optimum control of the suspect?

- How is my physical **condition** and health? Is it better than the suspect's? How does this affect my approach?

- What's my **state** of mind? Am I focused or am I distracted? Do I feel uneasy or am I too confident? Can I easily read the suspect's face to see his intentions?

- How's my **position** compared to the suspect? Is he shorter or taller than me? How are the suspect's hands positioned? Could he be concealing a weapon?

- How am I presenting myself to the suspect? Is my **stance** correct? Or will my weak **posture** leave me off-balance if the suspect launches an attack?

These questions help the police officer understand his relative position and decide on how he should act. If the officer decides that he can't read the suspect's intentions or movements because of how dark it is outside, his best relative position is probably at a distance where he can control the man with a weapon and wait for backup. But because situations evolve constantly during conflicts, the officer must always be prepared to change his relative position. The suspect may decide to take hostile action at the outset of the fight and close the distance between himself and the officer. Now, the officer must quickly reconsider his relative position and act to maintain the advantage. In this case, the officer moves backward to gain more reaction time to deal with the suspect because it's better for him to maintain his distance until he figures out whether the suspect's armed and why he's charging.

Calculating your relative position under stressful circumstances requires practice. Israeli Special Forces units, for instance, learn how to consider and deal with variables that can affect their relative position until it becomes second nature. Yet, it's important to understand that the questions, elements and variables a person learns to consider depend entirely on the individual because civilians, police officers and soldiers rarely prepare for the same encounters. Instead, they must all consider their own abilities and experiences to determine which techniques and positions will work best for them during a fight. In fact, true masters of this principle will begin considering their relative position from the moment they wake up in the morning, long before any conflict begins. It is simply their second nature to take into account every factor that could affect their safety every time they leave their homes.

Kapap has made relative position an integral part of its current system because the principle is flexible and benefits practitioners of any skill level. Because kapap borrows techniques and principles from many systems, students will always have the necessary tools to gain the best position during a fight. Also, kapap puts a great deal of emphasis on the first move of a fight because it will determine the combat options for the conflict's duration.

To prepare their students, kapap instructors throw as many variables at them as possible through realistic and creative exercises. Kapap instructors train their students in potential conflict locations, which can include stairways, elevators, parking lots and cars. An instructor might also momentarily blind his students with flashbulbs or strobe lights to imitate conflicts in which they can't see, or he may have them fight in water to overcome a natural human fear. Because fights never go completely as planned, kapap instructors want their students to be able to make quick decisions to assess their relative position when real conflict breaks outs. Basically, by taking their students out of a sterile environment, instructors help them become more confident and self-reliant.

This chapter will show you how to gain the advantage in a fight by being aware of your relative position. For instructors looking for inspiration, get to know your students' abilities and backgrounds. For students, don't be afraid to roll on the ground or fight near obstacles. Also don't expect instant success because training is a gradual process that will help keep you safe during conflicts.

Relative Position and Basic Ground Defense

The ground is a good place to start learning about relative position because it helps beginners overcome their fear of being thrown or hit. Because it is an integral part of many traditional combat arts, martial artists may be familiar with the Brazilian jiu-jitsu techniques discussed in this chapter. Security, law-enforcement and VIP-protection personnel, on the other hand, might find this training difficult because they are taught to never fight on the ground unless they have backup. Even if you've never done any ground work, you could still find yourself unarmed and fighting for your life on the ground. Whatever your combat background, however, remember that real safety in conflict depends on simple skills that address every facet of defense.

In the following sections, Avi Nardia and John Machado demonstrate how relative position works on the ground.

Relative Position With John Machado
Starting Position

In the above situation, John Machado (left) is in a weak relative position compared to Ahmed Best (right). Machado's ground movements are limited and so are his options because Best is on top and has more mobility (1). To change that, Machado slides his hips to the side of his opponent, which is a small movement that will have big implications for the outcome of the conflict. Now that Best is no longer directly over him, Machado can put his arm around the rear of his opponent's midsection (2). Because of this small movement, Machado has put himself in a position to gain a more dominant hold on the fight through a variety of techniques.

To illustrate this, take a look at Machado's options now that he is in a better relative position:

OPTION 1: Sweep Takedown or Balance Displacement

Once Machado has moved to the side and placed his arm around his opponent's body, he uses his right leg to push and his left arm to pull Best (1). Because Machado's right leg is pushing against Best's down-T, a balance displacement is caused, which will pull both grapplers in a circular motion. In the process of this motion, Best will end up on the ground (2), while Machado will end up in an upright position, which is also the more controlling of the two (3-4). Note that a "sweep takedown" is the correct term in jiu-jitsu, while "balance displacement" is the correct term in kapap.

OPTION 2: Armbar Defense

As he slides his hips to the side, Machado holds on to Best's arm (1). He then rocks back and swings his leg over Best's head (2-3). With his head pinned to the side and his right arm locked between Machado's knees, Best can't move (4). Notice how Best can only target and hit Machado's legs with his left hand; he can't launch a countermove (5). In his more dominant position, Machado also could hyperextend his opponent's elbow, causing it to break, by bringing his knees together (6).

Chapter 4

OPTION 3: Rear Mount Defense

In this Brazilian jiu-jitsu move, Machado forces Best to the ground by climbing on top of him (1-3). When in his new position, Machado uses balance displacement to force Best to the ground (4-5). The displacement occurs when Machado is fully on top of his opponent. At the end, Machado immobilizes Best with a rear-naked choke (6).

OPTION 4: The Elevator

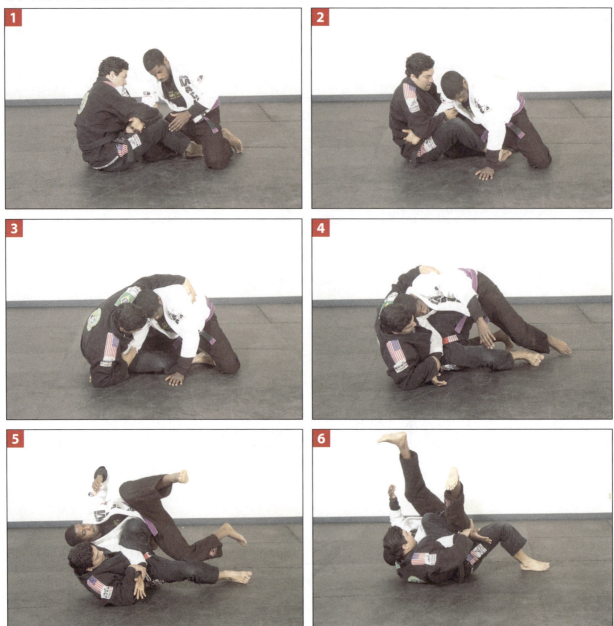

Machado locks Best into place with his arm and leg (1-2). He pushes Best's left knee with his right foot and pulls at his opponent's shoulder with his left arm (3). He then knocks Best off-balance (4). The balance displacement caused by Machado lifting Best up and over is the reason this move is called the "elevator" (5-6).

Note: When you begin training for relative position, you must go slowly. The picture sequence only captures one of Machado's decisions to reposition himself and dominate his opponent. During a real grappling session, Machado would actually need to constantly re-evaluate his relative position in order to counter Best's moves.

OPTION 5: Butterfly Guard

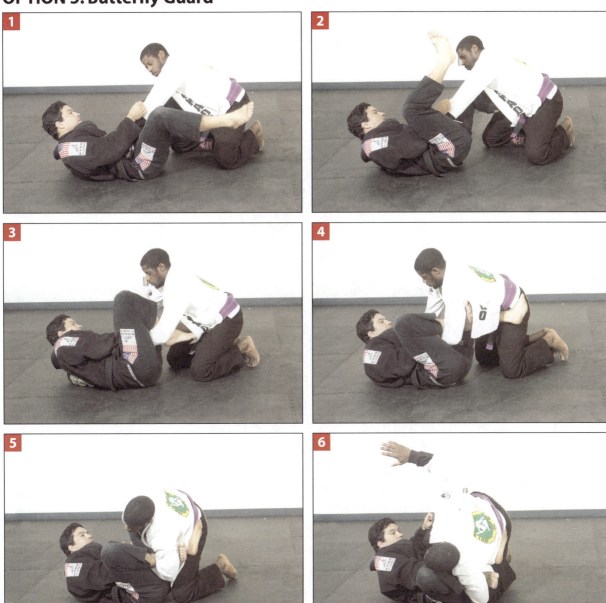

In this ground position, Machado uses a variation of the "butterfly guard" (feet between the opponent's legs) to trap Best's elbows and body in place (1-3). Even from this position, Machado has a variety of choices to gain a more advantageous position. In this case, he knocks Best off-balance by pulling on Best's arm and pushing Best's gut with his legs (4-6). Note: It's important to train for balance and performance, which will make it easier for you to decide which moves you can use in a real conflict.

Relative Position With Avi Nardia
Starting Position

Avi Nardia (bottom), a kapap trainer, finds himself in a disadvantageous position against his attacker. Student Scott Seroll has nailed him to the floor by using a tracheal pressure point. There are a variety of ways for Nardia to shift his position into one that will help him control his opponent and the outcome of the fight.

One basic difference between the following options and the Brazilian jiu-jitsu ones mentioned previously is that kapap is reality-based and prepares students for scenarios in which they must fight for their life. While Brazilian jiu-jitsu and other martial arts are still relevant to dynamic conflicts for their tactics, many such practices have become competition sports. This is why Machado maintains contact with his opponent to hold him in place, such as in a grappling tournament, while Nardia seeks to put distance between himself and Seroll, such as in a real-life ambush. Distance will also give Nardia more reaction time to judge what his next relative position should be. In the end, kapap is for self-defense, not grappling tournaments. The kapap goal is safety and escape.

Here's what Nardia can do in order to get out of Seroll's choke hold and dominate the fight:

OPTION 1: Eye Jab With Sweep

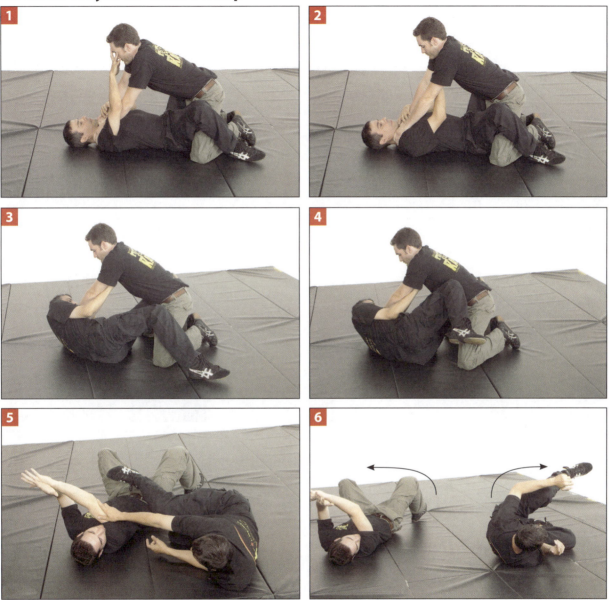

To change his relative position, Nardia gouges his attacker's eyes (1). In a real situation, attackers that are high on drugs or alcohol may not let go when their eyes are attacked. That's why Nardia quickly reassesses his relative position and then strikes at Seroll's trachea (2). When this does not work, Nardia slides his hips out from under the attacker before performing a scissor sweep to unbalance him (3-5). This rolls the attacker in one direction, giving Nardia an opportunity to escape by rolling away (6). Even though several of his techniques failed, Nardia was able to change to a better relative position because his training and experience have given him a number of tools.

OPTION 2: Kangaroo Kick

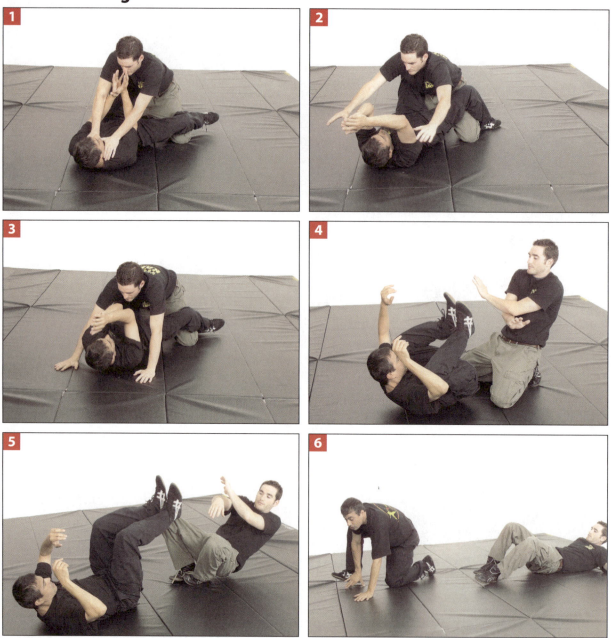

To change his relative position, Nardia brings his arms up and drives them backward (1-2). This not only releases Nardia from the choke hold but also causes his opponent to fall forward. When Seroll catches his fall, he immediately needs to pull back in order to avoid an impact with Nardia's upheld elbows (3). When Seroll tries to regain balance, Nardia kangaroo kicks his attacker in the chest, which finally gives him the opportunity to get away (4-6).

OPTION 3: Head Rotation or Manipulation on the Ground

To break Seroll's choke hold, Nardia brings his arms up and drives them through his attacker's arms (1). The move catches Seroll off-guard and knocks him off-balance, causing him to drop his hands to the floor and change his relative position. Nardia then shifts and strikes the attacker with his elbows (2). With his opponent distracted, Nardia reaches around the back of Seroll's neck and grabs his hair and jaw (3). He then twists Seroll off with a push-pull in order to escape (4-6).

OPTION 4: Hand Traps

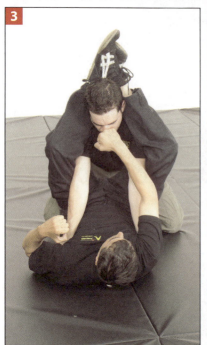
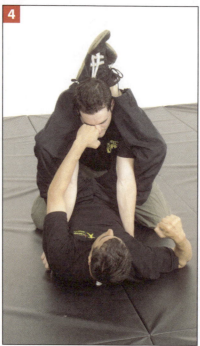

Mixing jiu-jitsu techniques with kapap principles, Nardia catches Seroll's head with his legs and crosses his feet so that his attacker can't escape (1). From here, Nardia has several options. First, he can decide to hold the attacker in place until help arrives. Second, he can break his attacker's arms, which will allow him to escape, by arching his back and pulling Seroll's wrists outward (2). Third, he can pull Seroll's hands forward and trap them between his armpits (3). From this position, Nardia can apply punches (4) or even an eye gouge (5), which would also lead to an escape.

Chapter 4

Relative Position in Other Ground Scenarios

Here are some other ground positions that demonstrate relative position in law enforcement, kapap and Brazilian jiu-jitsu.

SCENARIO 1: Virgin Guard

Avi Nardia attacks kapap instructor Tad Nelson, who is armed with a gun (1). In an attempt to keep the weapon out of Nardia's reach, Nelson moves his gun under his hip instead of bringing it up to his chest to fire at his attacker (2-5). After he has moved it into position, Nelson fires (6). This ground-defense technique can be used to handle other scenarios. For example, a woman who is pinned to the ground by a rapist can reach a hand under her hip to attack her assaulter's groin rather than claw at his face.

SCENARIO 2: Escape From Guard Position—Kapap Style

Unlike the previous examples, Nardia is now in an upright position. However, his relative position is still weak enough that he can't escape without seriously endangering his safety (1). To change that, Nardia strikes at Scott Seroll in the trachea or face (2-3). Despite the fact that these are sensitive areas, Seroll refuses to loosen his leg hold, which means Nardia is still in a weak position. Next, Nardia pins his attacker to the ground by putting weight on Seroll's biceps with his arms locked (4). This effectively immobilizes the top half of the attacker's body. Nardia then pushes his head into his attacker's solar plexus (5). By putting pressure on Seroll's gut, Nardia not only restricts Seroll's ability to breathe but also can use this opportunity to stand up (6). While he rises, Nardia maintains pressure on the solar plexus, which will make it difficult for Seroll to maintain his leg hold (7). Once upright, Nardia continues to control his position by putting pressure on Seroll's groin, or he can move to a safer distance (8-9). Now if he is attacked, Nardia is in a position to kick back.

KAPAP: Combat Concepts

SCENARIO 3: Escape From Guard Position—Brazilian Jiu-Jitsu Style

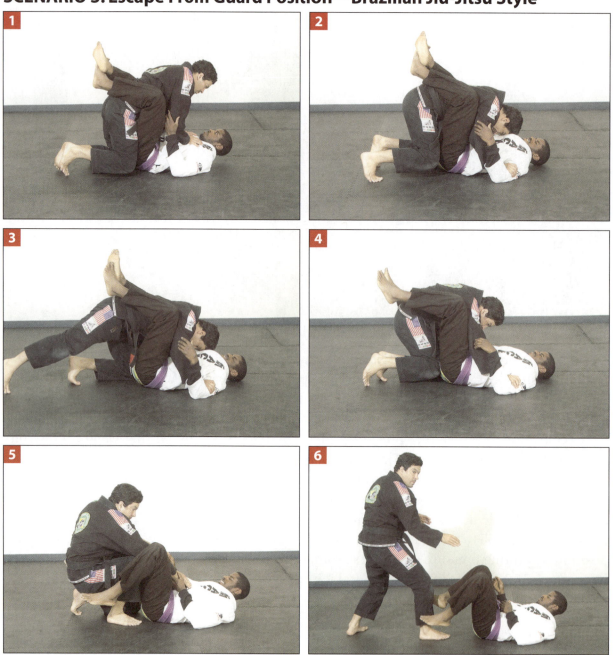

John Machado and Ahmed Best demonstrate a Brazilian jiu-jitsu technique that was assimilated into kapap (1). Because Machado is on top, he puts pressure on Best's solar plexus, which acts as an immobilizer (2-3). Now that his opponent is stunned, Machado can stand up and face him with a new attack (4-6). In truth, any technique from any discipline is valid in a real-life conflict as long as it is effective and works for the individual performing it.

Relative Position and Basic Standing Defenses

In standing defenses, the best way to see how relative position works is through the "Frankenstein" technique. (See Page 68.) However, the following sequences will demonstrate how Avi Nardia uses relative position to his advantage in certain upright conflict situations.

Starting Position

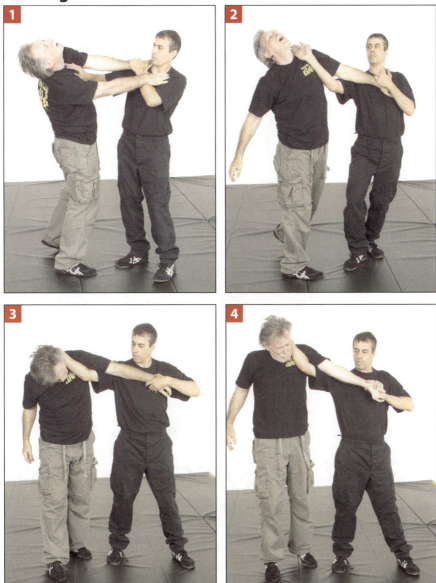

Kapap stresses the first movement as the most important, but in a real conflict, that isn't always the case. Here, Nardia faces his opponent while in a choke hold (1). From this weak position, Nardia does a standard armbar technique in order to handle the conflict (2-4). Now, he has several options for how to proceed.

OPTION 1: Takedown During an Escape

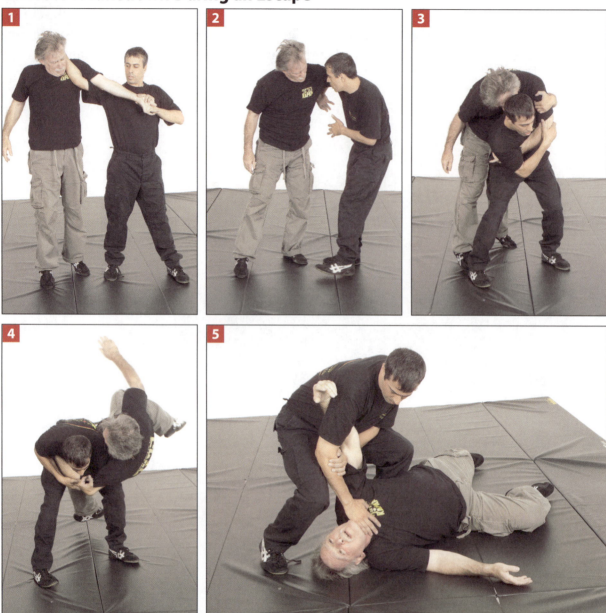

This time, the attacker changes his relative position by pulling himself free from the armbar (1-2). Nardia quickly reacts and changes his position to execute a judo takedown on his opponent (3-4). He then controls his attacker with an arm lock (5) or could finish him with the "Elvis" technique. (See Page 48.)

Chapter 4

OPTION 2: Head Lock and Takedown

Using balance dispacement and the principle of two points of contact, Nardia steps back while pulling his attacker's left arm to the floor, which takes the man to the ground (1-2). Nardia then applies an arm and wrist lock with his legs to control the attacker (3). From this position, Nardia can use the "Elvis" technique (4). (See Page 48.)

KAPAP: Combat Concepts

FINISHING MANEUVER 1: "Elvis" From a Standing Position

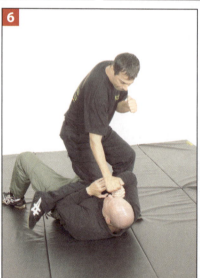
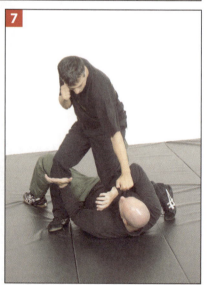

From the takedown mentioned in the previous sequence, Nardia can transition into the "Elvis" technique—a common kapap defense (1-2). In the "Elvis," Nardia straddles his opponent's ribs and twists his hips like the famous rock star (3-5). Nardia can strike his attacker multiple times with his legs or knees, or he can squeeze the man's ribs until the opponent suffocates (6-7).

FINISHING MANEUVER 2: "Elvis" From a Mount Position

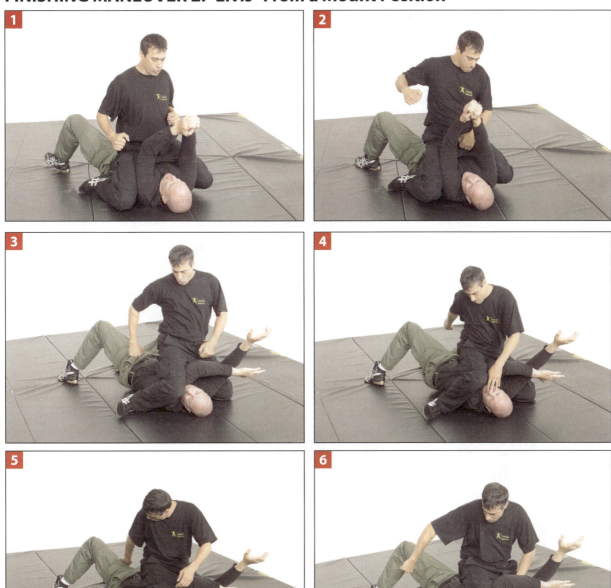

Depending on your personal tastes or strength, the "Elvis" technique can also be executed from a mount position. This means that you can use your hands to hit an opponent's face, groin or ribs in order to keep him in place (1-3). While sitting on his opponent's chest, Nardia thrusts his hips up and down, which not only knocks the air out of the opponent's lungs but also makes it easier for Nardia to strike his opponent's face and groin (4-6).

Relative Position and Attacks From the Front (Counters and Releases)

Similar to how a Brazilian jiu-jitsu fighter moves around his opponent on the floor, a kapap practitioner must learn how to position and move around an opponent while standing. This section covers how relative position might play out in a frontal assault.

OPTION 1: Controlled Side Applications

Avi Nardia lifts up his arms to block a frontal attack, steps toward his opponent and elbows him in the face (1-2). A common kapap principle is the high-low-high triangle. (See Page 22.) Nardia uses this principle by striking his opponent high in the face before distracting him with a low strike to the groin (2-3). Before the attacker can decide what to do or where to move next, Nardia surprises him with another high attack (4). Basically, like a gyroscope, Nardia always keeps his opponent unsure of his next movement (5). From here, Nardia has several options for finishing his attack and escaping.

Chapter 4

FINISHING MANEUVER 1: Armbar

Nardia straightens his left arm and pulls his opponent into an armbar from which he can execute standing moves. (See Page 45.)

FINISHING MANEUVER 2: Armbar and Groin Strike

As an alternative, Nardia pulls his attacker's arm over his shoulder to apply an armbar (1) and strike him in the groin (2).

KAPAP: Combat Concepts

OPTION 2: Head Rotation and Takedown

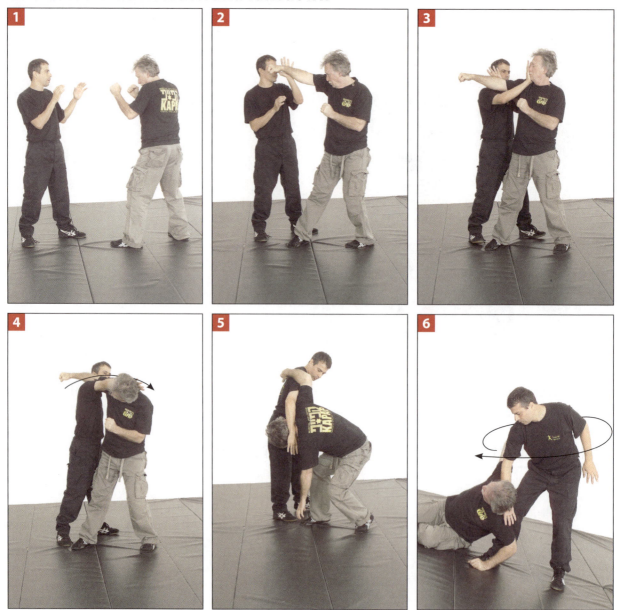

While the controlled side-application technique uses movements similar to those found in traditional martial arts, Nardia uses boxing techniques in this one. He faces his opponent with his hands at ready (1). When his opponent strikes, Nardia blocks the punch like a boxer (2). He then uses more traditional martial arts movements by stepping in and placing his right hand behind his attacker's neck (3-4). Next, he uses the gyro principle (See Page 22.) to force his attacker to the ground by disorienting him through movement (5-6).

OPTION 3: Release From a Hold and Trapping

Nardia's opponent changes his relative position by bringing Nardia into a wrestling clinch (1). Nardia immediately moves to a stronger relative position by grabbing the attacker's right wrist, hitting his groin, then striking his nose (2-3). Because the attacker is confused by the low/high attack, Nardia can twist his right arm and, even though it is not shown, sweep him to the floor (4-6).

OPTION 4: Hair Pull

The attacker grabs Nardia by the hair (1). Instead of thrashing his head back and forth, Nardia pulls his head downward to unbalance his attacker (2). He then steps to the side and puts pressure on his attacker's elbow with his own (3). The conflict is ended with a restraint or finishing technique from any discipline (4). In this case, Nardia uses an arm and wrist lock to end the conflict and escape.

Chapter 4

Relative Position and Attacks From the Rear (Counters and Releases)

In the following examples, Avi Nardia demonstrates some options for relative position when attacked from the rear.

OPTION 1: Tiger Mouth

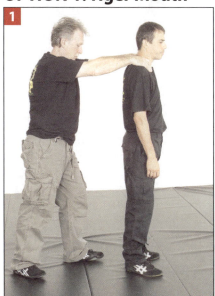

An attacker grabs Nardia from behind (1). Nardia steps sideways to create enough room to hit his attacker low in the groin (2). He then circles his right arm upward and outward in a butterfly circle to make his attacker release his grip (3). After that, he can follow up his high arm arc with a low attack to the groin or a high attack to the face, which traps the opponent's right hand under his armpit (4). The finishing technique is called the "tiger mouth" because it resembles a technique of the same name in Okinawan karate.

OPTION 2: Gross-Motor Moves

When an attacker grabs Nardia from behind, he turns sideways and attacks his opponent in the face or the groin (1-3). Nardia then circles his right arm so it locks his attacker's arm and forces him off-balance (4-5). He follows up with a strike to the groin and applies a "masking" technique (See Page 93.), which forces the attacker to the ground (6-7). Nardia subdues his attacker with a restraining or finishing technique (8).

Relative Position With Partners

Most close-quarters combat systems like to divide things into threes because it's easy to remember, and kapap is no exception. When working with partners or in a team, think of yourself as part of a triangle or "V," and recognize how your movements affect your relative position as compared to your opponents <u>and</u> your teammates. Your relative position not only must give you an advantage over your opponent but also must help your partner.

In the following example, kapap trainers Avi Nardia (far right) and Albert Timen move in to arrest a hostile suspect. After that, we'll also consider how partners must use relative position in more specialized scenarios beyond a simple arrest.

SCENARIO 1: Suspect Search by Avi Nardia and Albert Timen

Forming a "V," Nardia and Timen flank a hostile suspect and secure the area so that he can't escape (1). Nardia isn't armed here because he will perform the arrest, but Timen is armed because he must cover the suspect and ensure everyone's safety. Following orders, the suspect goes to the wall and spreads his arms and legs (2). When Nardia moves in for the arrest, Timen also moves closer so that his reaction time will be fast enough if something happens (3).

Because Nardia's standing to the right of the suspect while he searches him, Timen positions himself to the left so he has a clean shot at the suspect (4). When Nardia switches sides, Timen crosses over to the opposite side so that the team still maintains full control of the situation (5-6).

SCENARIO 2: VIP-Protection Simulation With Two Bodyguards

In this VIP-protection simulation, there are four people: the VIP, bodyguard A (Ahmed Best), bodyguard B (John Machado) and an attacker (1). When the scenario begins, the attacker rushes bodyguard A, so bodyguard B covers the VIP (2). Even though both teammates are doing their job, they aren't working as a team because bodyguard A can't see what bodyguard B is doing. Likewise, bodyguard B can't help his partner subdue the attacker, so he moves to the side where both partners will create a triangle with the opponent (3). They both flank the downed suspect and the door.

In a triangle or "V" shape position, both bodyguards can now protect the VIP and deal with new attackers (4). When a new attacker enters, bodyguard B prepares to fire at him, knowing that his partner is safe and the initial opponent is subdued (5). Meanwhile, bodyguard A can ensure that the first attacker doesn't retaliate, and he also is in a position to help his partner, if necessary (6).

KAPAP: Combat Concepts

SCENARIO 3: VIP-Protection Simulation With Three Bodyguards

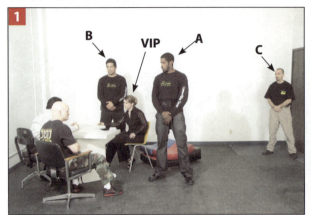

In this simulated meeting, there are six people: a VIP, one bystander, bodyguard A (Best), bodyguard B (Machado), bodyguard C (Timen) and an attacker (1). The three bodyguards are set up in a triangular formation to protect the VIP. Bodyguards A and B stand next to the sitting VIP, while bodyguard C stands next to the door. In the middle of the meeting, an attacker stands up and lunges toward the VIP (2). Bodyguard A moves to take care of the attacker while bodyguard B—who clearly sees his teammate engage the opponent—moves to cover the VIP (3). During the altercation, bodyguard B removes the VIP from the room (4-8).

Notice the layered team effort. Bodyguard A is fully engaged in hand-to-hand combat with the attacker. Bodyguard B is fully aware of the conflict and can help, if necessary, but must watch the bystander and move the VIP to safety. Meanwhile, bodyguard C understands all the dynamics from his position and can either help bodyguard A or B take down the attacker, remove the VIP from the room or cover the bystander.

****

Whether you want to maintain contact or escape, understanding relative position will help you control a conflict. Training is essential because it shows you what positions and moves apply to your experiences and work best with your mind and body. Interacting with a variety of partners, strategies and scenarios can also help you create an effective combat game because your training partners serve as live "dummies" who will help you learn what positions are best for you. While this chapter gives you a variety of options, you must go beyond the exercises in the book and increase the difficulty of your relative-position training on your own.

CHAPTER 5: CONDITIONING

When conditioning comes to mind, most people think of getting in shape, but kapap exercises—whether they are for warming up, stretching or strength training—often hold a higher purpose. Instead of performing rote movements in a set fashion, kapap combat-conditioning exercises not only help you physically but also prepare you mentally for conflicts through stress training.

For example, a man trains to do 100 continuous push-ups. While this is an admirable goal, being able to do 100 push-ups will not help him if he is randomly attacked and must fight for his life. Of course, the exercise will improve his health, but it won't help him develop combat skills. In contrast, a kapap practitioner considers how he can improvise, create and tailor his conditioning activities not only to increase his combat skills but also to use them as battle-ready positions. Rather than doing push-ups for the sake of push-ups, a kapap practitioner does push-ups to upgrade the skills in his "toolbox."

The key to remember about kapap conditioning, and really any aspect of kapap, is that creativity is essential. As a mixed martial art, kapap takes the knowledge and wisdom accumulated from past disciplines, then assimilates them into effective principles and techniques for modern settings. This means that your current conditioning routine doesn't have to change. The question is, How can you use conditioning to make sure you are 100-percent prepared to defend yourself?

To help you answer that, the following exercises can be tailored to increase your physical and mental endurance. This chapter will also discuss how exercises that are not rote lead to "muscle confusion." By training with a variety of exercises and routines instead of only one, every day, you "confuse" your muscles. They won't become accustomed to one movement or one form of exercise, and this will help diversify your mobility, balance and control of movements. In addition, while it's always better to set up a conditioning routine that works best for you, a general guideline to start with is to do most of these exercises in five sets of three-minute rounds with a one-minute rest in between.

Mobility Exercises

Mobility exercises are important because mobility is just as relevant as power in a fight; it allows you to transition quickly between techniques and positions. In order to train for it, a jump-rope is a versatile piece of equipment that can be used for many conditioning and mobility exercises. The following are a few examples of how easy it is to make a rope a vital part of your conditioning routine.

Chapter 5

OPTION 1: Jumping Rope

At its most basic, skipping rope is a great cardio activity that increases your stamina. However, don't just skip over the rope because you don't want your body to become accustomed to just one movement. Mix up the routine by doing things like running in place (1-2), rotating while you jump (3) and doing high jumps (4). This training and these triggers will help you develop well-rounded hand-eye coordination and increase your stamina.

OPTION 2: Shadowboxing

In this exercise, two trainers hold a long rope and move it up and down and side to side. While they do this, the student shadowboxes and jumps over and under the rope to increase his physical endurance (1-6). Throughout the entire exercise, the student must try to avoid touching the rope. The student must watch his balance to quickly cope with the rope's movements.

There are many ways to vary this conditioning exercise for students with different skill levels. For instance, beginners can either shadowbox or jump over and under a stationary rope to gradually increase their physical strength.

OPTION 3: Dry Fire and Stationary Turns

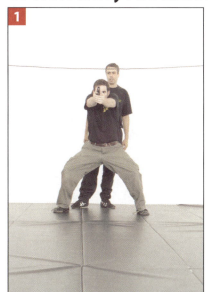

This training exercise uses a rope and a firearm, which should <u>not</u> be loaded for safety reasons. In this stress-training scenario, the rope simulates obstacles that the student must maneuver around to get a clear shot (1-3). Two instructors or students hold the rope steady during the exercise (4). However, they could also move it up and down or side to side to increase the level of difficulty.

OPTION 4: The Frankenstein

If you don't have a rope, use this conditioning and mobility exercise favored by the Kapap Academy. Like Frankenstein's monster, the kapap instructor holds his arms out in front of him while his student throws air punches that do not connect with their target (1-4). To increase the difficulty of the exercise and make it more dynamic, the instructor swings his arms randomly (5-12). The student, meanwhile, must avoid his teacher's moving arms by ducking, dodging and blocking while he tries to score "hits." Like the rope exercises mentioned previously, the student must deal with a stationary or moving obstacle. This time, the obstacle is more difficult because the person can move any way he likes.

Stretching

In kapap, stretches are performed while moving so you can increase your flexibility and agility at the same time. You'll also be able to control and move into more advantageous positions during a fight with quicker movements. Stretching can also help you transition into other positions that could be used to launch combat techniques. As a plausible battle-ready position, each stretch acts as a path to increase the "tools" you have at ready in a fight.

Here are some ideas on how to incorporate movement into common stretching exercises.

OPTION 1: Groin Stretch

A simple groin stretch—standing with your legs apart while shifting your weight to one side with a bent knee—helps loosen muscles, but a groin stretch with movement improves balance, reduces risk of injuries and can help you retreat from a ground position in a fight. When stretching forward, don't bend your knee too far beyond your ankle (1). When stretching backward, make sure your hip and knee line up with your ankle (2). Use controlled, smooth movements rather than fast or jerky ones to avoid injury.

OPTION 2: Calf Stretch

A regular calf stretch involves pushing back on your hands to stretch out the back of your leg. However, there are ways to improvise with this exercise. In the pictures above, the kapap student stretches his calf and then quickly switches to his other foot (1-2). In this way, he can use this simple stretch to transition into other conditioning exercises like push-ups, headstands or planks. He can also use it as a transition into another technique or relative position during a fight.

Remember to use controlled, smooth movements and keep your back flat and abs tight. Also, keep both knees slightly bent and unlocked to facilitate movement.

OPTION 3: Hip Stretch to Full-Body Stretch

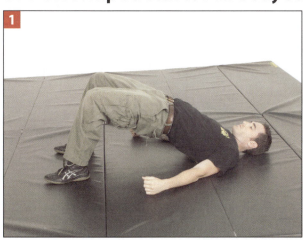

A simple hip stretch is an excellent way to loosen the muscles (1). From this standard stretch, the student would come down to the ground before transitioning into a full-body stretch (2). From a full-body stretch, he now has the option to practice a common position in Brazilian jiu-jitsu for grappling, which can throw an opponent off-balance. Make sure your abdominals are sufficiently warmed up before you attempt a full-body stretch!

KAPAP: Combat Concepts

OPTION 4: Abdominal Exercises

From a full-body stretch, you can also easily transition into abdominal exercises, which include crunches (1), bicycle crunches (2-3), "V" sit-ups (4) and side crunches (5). Crunches can also help you prepare for battle-ready positions. For example, if a police officer is thrown to the ground, he must get up. Using his abdominal muscles, he crunches up into a sitting position and draws his gun to take down his attacker. In regards to "V" sit-ups, be careful of lower back pain; only lift your legs to a height that does not cause physical discomfort.

Again, your fitness level should influence how you set up your conditioning, and there are many ways to enhance your physical and mental stress training beyond this book. For example, with abdominal exercises, you could use a medicine ball during crunches or condition with a partner.

Strengthening Exercises

Strengthening exercises not only improve your power but also your balance, agility and reaction time. Because kapap is about learning how to "fight for your life," practitioners train to become stronger and more dynamic.

OPTION 1: Squats and Lunges

Many martial arts and combat systems launch attacks from both the lunge (1) and squat (2) positions. That's why it's important to condition yourself for these battle-ready stances. Doing squats and lunges also increases your balance and leg strength, both of which will help you move into relative positions of control during a fight. To enhance your stress training, use a medicine ball or other weights for added resistance. In order to confuse your muscles, you can switch from a lunge to a squat position at random intervals.

OPTION 2: Leg and Kick

This exercise, which is common in Brazilian jiu-jitsu and wrestling, starts in a crouch position and stretches out each leg with a kick (1). From there, you return to a crouch position (2) and then kick out your leg in the opposite direction (3). To mix up the movements and increase your stamina through stress conditioning, add push-ups or other exercises. Don't use the same number of repetitions every time. Instead, improvise and mix up your conditioning routine to stay loose and ready for anything.

OPTION 3: Neck Exercise

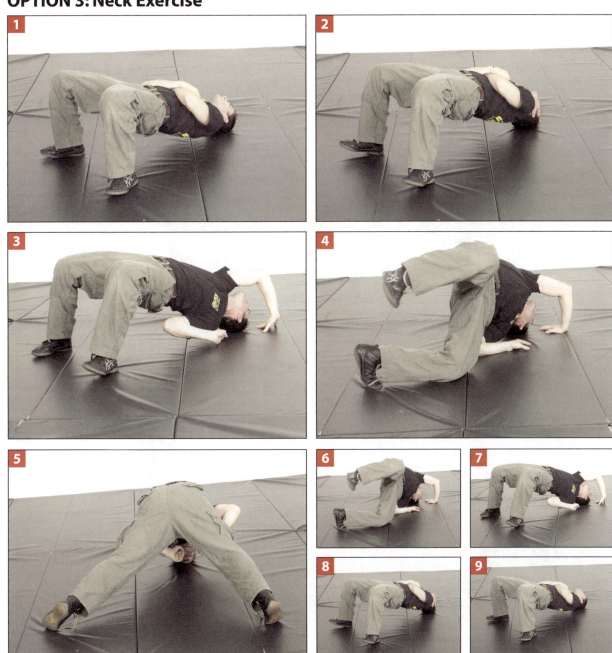

To strengthen your neck, slowly bridge your body (1-2). Then slowly rotate your body—shoulders, torso and hips (3-5). When you are looking at the ground, repeat the same movement in the opposite direction until you have returned to your original position (6-9). The start of this exercise is similar to the hip stretch and full-body stretch mentioned earlier. It also requires extreme caution, and only advanced practitioners should attempt it. However, you can still improvise different transitions and movements that will work for your current physical level.

OPTION 4: Sit-Ups Into Standing Position

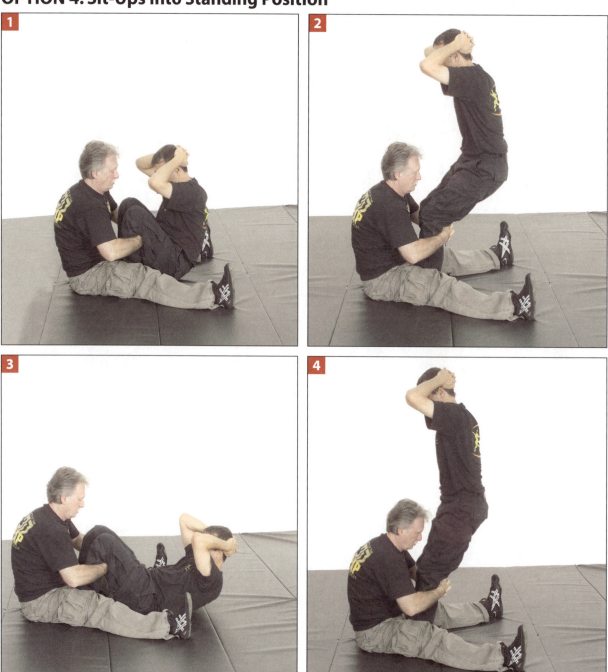

There are many types of sit-ups. However, the skills used for this sit-up are easily transferable to combat. In a ground fight, you may have to do this move to escape, like when in a ground-defense or grappling position. To train for the possibility, a trainer holds the legs of a student while he does a sit-up into a standing position (1-4). Again, you can increase stress training by using a medicine ball or adding more moves to make the exercise a combination.

OPTION 5: Push-Ups

Push-ups not only add to your "toolbox" of dynamic moves but also help improve balance and increase strength and physical endurance. Certain push-up variations can also strengthen body parts that are usually forgotten, like the fingers. These variations include but are not limited to fingertip push-ups (1), ballistic push-ups with midair hand claps (2), one-handed push-ups that switch from hand to hand (3-4), knuckle push-ups (5) and diamond push-ups (6).

OPTION 6: Leopard Crawl/Tiger Walk

This technique is called the tiger walk or leopard crawl because of its feline movements. It starts in a push-up position. From there, the kapap practitioner brings a leg forward, as if he is going to crawl, while maintaining the push-up position (1). Next, he crawls forward by bringing one leg forward and then the other (2-3). He also moves his hands forward to maintain the fluidity of the crawling motion (4). This movement not only increases stamina and physical strength but also helps practitioners build up their grip strength for possible scenarios that involve climbing.

Chapter 5

Impact Conditioning

Training in the classroom rarely prepares a fighter for how a strike or kick will feel during a real conflict. That is a potential danger, especially in a random attack, because you don't want to be distracted by the pain. This is why impact training is so important. The following exercises will give you ideas on how to simulate impacts through reality-based stress conditioning. Impact training will also be discussed in Chapter 6.

OPTION 1: Simple Cardio

These partners are both conditioning their bodies and learning what a real impact feels like while doing cardio exercises. Because this is still training, the kicks are not thrown at full power. Instead, the "attacking" partner (left) holds his leg or foot up next to his intended target (1-3). As he balances in that position, he pushes at his partner, who will feel how his body is affected by the impact (2-4). The attacking partner will also see how his kick will affect a potential opponent. These exercises aren't supposed to be like breaking boards in martial arts. Instead, they are conditioning exercises meant to increase and help you understand the potential power in combat through cardio and impact training.

OPTION 2: Absorb-Thrust Drill

Stand approximately 10 feet apart (1) and throw a medicine ball at your partner's chest (2). Your partner should catch the ball directly on his chest (3). He then throws the medicine ball back to his partner (4). This exercise simulates real impacts and helps strengthen your body to absorb blows during a real conflict. Your skill level should also dictate the distance, weight and strength with which you throw the ball.

OPTION 3: Medicine-Ball Boxing

Even if he's a fantastic fighter, a boxer could be at a disadvantage in a real fight because he's used to throwing punches with his gloves on. This means he could seriously hurt his hand if he struck an opponent while gloveless. To overcome that, he can condition creatively. In this sequence, a trainer holds a medicine ball while his student moves around and strikes it with various punches (1-4). Because this is a kapap conditioning activity, both partners benefit from the training. The student who's boxing learns what a real impact feels like on his fist, while the trainer's stomach is conditioned because it absorbs the impacts taken directly by the medicine ball.

OPTION 4: Head-Butt Sit-Ups

This drill combines several conditioning exercises and strengthens your neck muscles. The student is in a sit-up position, which works his abdominals, and he is also in a stress situation because he must hit the falling soccer ball with his head (1-3). The trainer also improves his coordination by balancing on the student's feet and holding them in place while he tosses the ball. If the exercise is too difficult, the student can use a medicine ball to toss to the trainer while doing sit-ups (4).

OPTION 5: Free Fall

The trainer drops a medicine ball on his student's stomach so that he will know what a strike to the gut feels like (1). In order to avoid getting hurt, the student tenses his abdominal muscles to absorb the impact and then throws the ball back to the trainer (2). The length of the drop depends on the student's abilities. If the student is advanced, the ball can be dropped from a greater height.

Knife Warm-Ups

When using a weapon, it's important to have a strong grip. This exercise, which uses rubber knives for safety, helps develop hand-eye coordination and increase mental awareness during a conflict.

OPTION 1: Basic Warm-Up

A trainer and a student stand 10 feet apart and throw a knife at varying heights and speeds to each other (1-2). To increase the difficulty, they can also alternate hands.

OPTION 2: Advanced Warm-Up

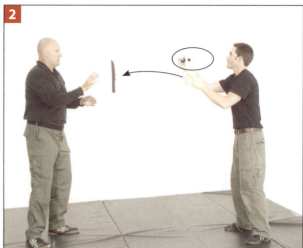

Because they have gradually upgraded their physical skills, the two practitioners are ready to move on to the next level. This time, they use two knives instead of one (1). In order to make the exercise more random, each partner tries to throw both knives at the same time to the other. In doing so, they increase the randomness of the exercise because the knives will not always be thrown in unison (2).

OPTION 3: Example Variations on Warm-Up

The kapap practitioners increase the difficulty and stress of the situation by standing on one leg for balance training (1). As they balance, the student throws both knives at his trainer and then vice versa. To increase the stress conditioning even more, they add the following rule: If either partner drops a knife while carrying out the knife drills, both do 10 push-ups (2).

Chapter 5

Group Conditioning

The following exercises are useful training drills for small or large groups like in a classroom.

OPTION 1: Random Throw

The trainer throws a medicine ball randomly to one of the students, who are lined up next to each other and moving in place randomly—bouncing, jogging, etc (1). The student throws the ball back to the instructor, who then tosses it to another student (2-3). This exercise not only boosts the students' physical endurance but also strengthens their hand-eye coordination while under stress.

OPTION 2: Pass Along

In this exercise, which typically requires two medicine balls, the students stand in a circle with their backs to one another. If there are more than four students, add another ball. The students pass the ball around in a circle quickly (1), and they even change direction from left to right and right to left (2). This helps them cope under pressure and strengthens their agility and grip.

OPTION 3: Ball Pass in a Circle

In this exercise, which also involves a ball toss, the students face each other in a circle with one of the students standing in the center (1). The student in the center throws the medicine ball to one of the students (2). He throws it back to the person in the middle who then throws it to another student (3). At all times, the middle person must remain aware of his environment and where everyone is. If there are a lot of students, this exercise can be performed with more than one ball and person in the middle.

OPTION 4: The Accordion Drill

The accordion drill describes the back-and-forth motion of this exercise. Standing between two trainers, a student strives to control the situation as best he can by punching (1, 5), kicking (2, 6), elbowing (3) or doing whatever it takes to keep the trainers away from him. The two trainers will pressure the situation by closing in on the student (3-4). The trainers can stay as close or far apart as is necessary to mimic the motion of an accordion and keep the student on his toes.

Chapter 5

****

In the end, all these drills and exercises are meant to increase and upgrade the tools in your "toolbox." They enhance physical skills, improve coordination, and toughen the body and spirit. Much more than a simple workout that burns calories, kapap conditioning prepares you to fight for your life. Remember to actively participate in your exercises—ask questions, improvise, be creative—because your abilities always depend on you to advance beyond your current skill level.

CHAPTER 6: THE ART OF IMPACT

Kapap defines "impact" as a force or shock that strikes a target. While this may seem like a simple statement for a powerful force, it remains an apt definition because it is all-inclusive. Rather than define impact as a kick or punch, kapap identifies impact as any force that can be applied by anything. This not only includes kicks and strikes but also defensive impacts, like blocks, or offensive impacts made by weapons, such as guns, sticks and knives. Because the definition is so broad, kapap practitioners are able to borrow techniques from a variety of systems to create their own well-rounded impact defense. In the case of the first Jewish settlers of Palestine, they chose to use sticks as impact weapons because they had very few self-defense options, whereas the modern kapap practitioner has many combat systems and martial arts from which to choose.

It's also important to remember that impact in kapap covers much more than just hitting your opponent. Instead, it requires knowledge, understanding and common sense. As a person aware of your relative position in life, do you know what impacts your body has been conditioned to withstand? Or do you know how strong of an impact you're capable of launching? In the end, impact in kapap is never about brute strength. Use your best weapon—your brain—to make the right choice during a close-quarters conflict to escape and live to fight another day.

This chapter gives you a taste of the variety of impacts out there. However, there is always more to learn, and this is just a starting point. One source will never give you a complete understanding of combat. Whether you're a student or an instructor, it's always important to find qualified teachers, educational outlets and other resources to add to your base of knowledge.

Pressure Points

When some people think about the concept of impact, they imagine a punch sending someone through a wall. However, an impact can be something as simple as a pressure-point attack, which is a powerful force applied to a small point on the body. Pressure-point techniques are also useful surprise techniques because they are located in areas of the body that most people consider to be part of their "personal space." This means that your opponent might not expect his personal space to be penetrated with a pressure-point technique, even during a real conflict. While pressure points might seem easy to learn, their effectiveness depends on the ability, skill, mental awareness and physical fitness of both the defender and attacker. For example, an opponent high on drugs might not know that he is being hit in a sensitive spot. If that happens, then it's best to consider your relative position and use a restraining technique instead.

OPTION 1: Nailing Techniques

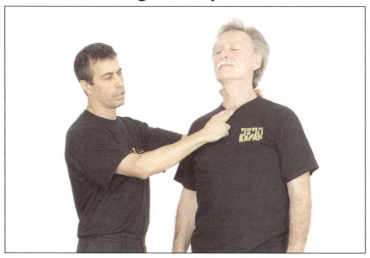

◀ Avi Nardia immobilizes his opponent by pressing his index and forefinger like a nail into his target, which is the larynx. Nailing techniques are extremely useful when you must hold your opponent up against a wall or down to the ground.

▶ Nardia uses another variation of the nailing technique by pressing three fingers down into the soft tissue between the collarbone and neck.

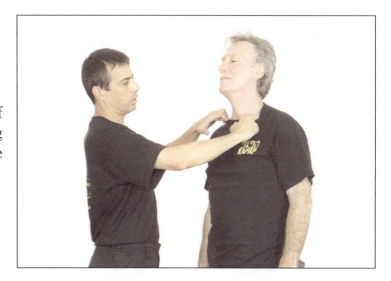

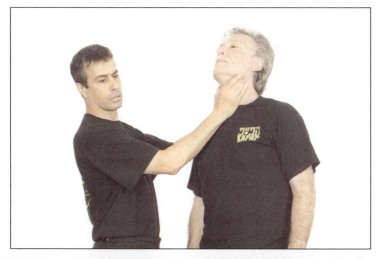

◀ In yet another variation of the nailing technique, Nardia wraps his hand around the larynx and presses up into the tissue just below the jaw line. Sometimes, this nailing technique is known as a "C" choke because of the shape of the defender's hand.

OPTION 2: Nailing Technique and Takedown

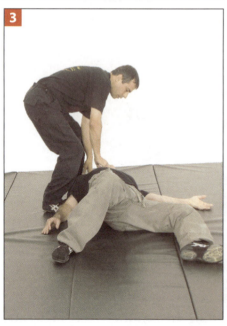

When you use impact force on a person's throat, his immediate natural reaction is to hunch over and protect the sensitive area. This technique takes advantage of that reaction. The opponent wants to hunch over, but Nardia pushes down on the pressure point, which forces the man to fall to the ground (1, 3). Nardia also takes advantage of the two-points-of-contact principle: When he pushes down on the pressure point, he also pushes up on his opponent's back with his free hand, forcing the man to lose his balance (2). When his opponent is finally on the floor, Nardia keeps him immobilized with the nailing technique and puts pressure on the man's ribs with his knee (4).

OPTION 3: Masking Technique or Applying the Mask

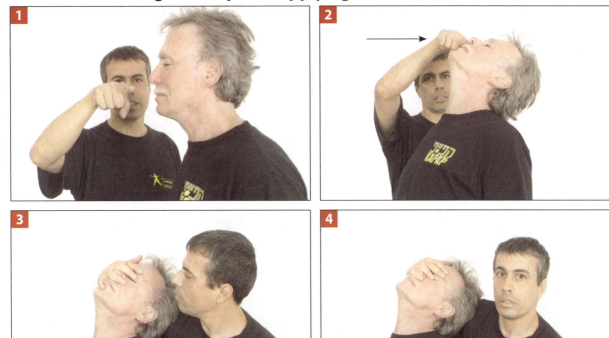

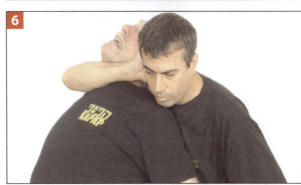

Though it may seem improbable, you can take down an opponent just with one finger. The masking technique uses the pressure point found under a person's nose to immobilize an attacker. In this sequence, Nardia applies pressure with his forefinger to a point just above his opponent's lip (1). This prevents the man from walking forward, but if he does, further pressure will force his head backward (2). The "mask" helps Nardia control the situation. With his opponent off-balance and uncertain because of the pressure-point technique, Nardia's hand masks his opponent's face (3). He can further control the situation by pressing into the man's eyes before taking him to the ground (4). Avoid masking an adversary between the lips because he might bite back. From a masking technique, Nardia can move into a rear choke hold, bringing his right arm under his opponent's chin and placing his right hand alongside his own head (5). Nardia then applies pressure by squeezing (6).

OPTION 4: Handshakes

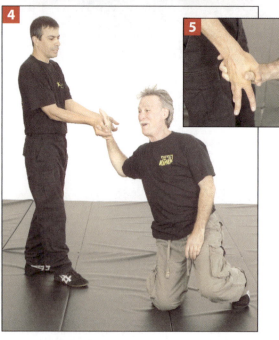

Using the two-points-of-contact principle, handshake techniques usually lead to armbars. In the above sequence, Nardia handles his attacker without an armbar by using a thumb lock. Initially, the technique looks like the two opponents are shaking hands (1). However, Nardia pushes his opponent off-balance by twisting his hand back and forth in the handshake grip (2-3). This forces the man to his knees. Nardia then applies the thumb lock (4). The pressure on the thumb will put the attacker under Nardia's control (5).

Sensor-Manipulation Strikes

Another overlooked form of impact is sensor manipulation. A defender can disable his opponent by distracting one of his five senses: sight, sound, taste, touch and smell. Because these impacts use small movements that can easily lead into other techniques, sensor-manipulation strikes can be considered an application of kapap's economy-of-motion principle.

OPTION 1: Key No. 1

An attacker performs a front choke hold on Avi Nardia (1). Instead of kicking, punching or struggling, Nardia strikes his opponent's ears with cupped palms because the shape of the hands traps air and makes the impact sound louder to the attacker's ears (2). Distracted by the noise and the unexpected attack against a sensitive area, the opponent can't defend against Nardia's knee strike to his groin (3).

OPTION 2: Key No. 2

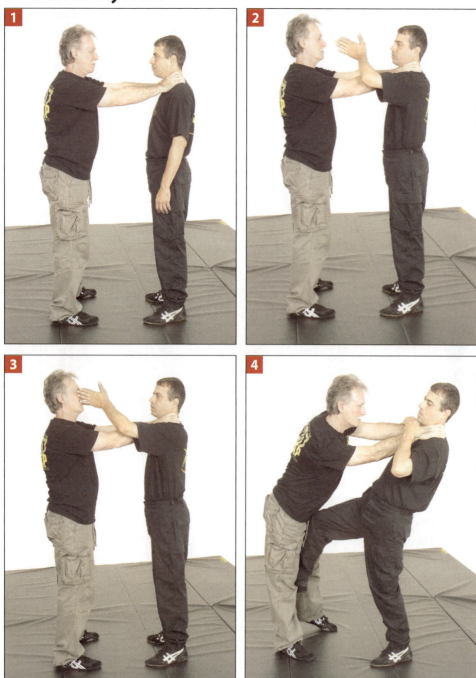

In this scenario, the opponent has Nardia in a front choke hold (1). Nardia distracts his attacker with a sudden clap, which makes the opponent blink and lose focus of the conflict for a brief moment (2). This gives Nardia the opportunity to launch a more potent attack, like an eye gouge (3). Like any move in kapap, there are numerous ways to use relative position with different impacts, which means that Nardia can also knee-strike the opponent in the groin as his finishing maneuver (4).

Chapter 6

Impact Conditioning

While impact plays an important role in any self-defense or combat system, training must be reality-based to properly prepare you for a real attack. Creative conditioning exercises force students to learn how to make an impact under stressful conditions and increase mobility, stamina and confidence. The following exercises will show you how to develop impact power through exercises that test your physical and mental endurance. During impact conditioning, combine and mix your punching and kicking techniques to encourage muscle confusion, which is explained in the previous chapter.

OPTION 1: Focus-Mitt Training

Ready Position

Left Jab

Right Cross

Left Uppercut

Right Uppercut

Left Hook

Left Leading Elbow

Right Elbow

Block With Left Elbow

Continued on next page

KAPAP: Combat Concepts

The student bobs and weaves while the instructor swings the mitts left and right (1-4).

In the pictures above and on the previous page, Scott Seroll and Tad Nelson do impact conditioning with focus mitts. Because the mitts are small, Seroll must be aware of his target and keep his movements under control, which helps him increase his stamina and focus. At the same time, Nelson learns how to properly absorb the impact through the focus mitts. He also moves the mitts to confuse the student and make striking the target more difficult.

OPTION 2: Thai-Pad Training

Right Roundhouse Kick

Right Cross

Left Roundhouse Kick

Right Knee

Left Knee

Right Elbow

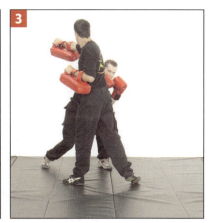

The instructor swings the pads at the head of the student, who must avoid being hit (1-3).

Thai pads are better for power impact training because they absorb shock more effectively than the less-padded and smaller focus mitts. In the pictures above, for example, a student develops her strikes, kicks and other technical elements while increasing her mental and physical endurance. Like with the focus-mitt training, her partner learns how to absorb the impacts and challenges her focus and mobility by moving the Thai pads around. However, he must also stay focused because his partner is using power techniques on these pads.

OPTION 3: Kick Shields

Left Jab

Right Cross

Right Front Kick

Right Push Kick

Left Roundhouse

Right Low Kick

The instructor uses the kick shield to hit his student when he rushes her (1-2). This forces her to stabilize herself against the impact and then move into a strong relative position for his next attack (3).

A quick kick to the pelvic area can drop even the most determined opponent, which is why kick shields are extremely effective for power training with speed. Because kick shields are heavier and more thickly padded, a student must use more power and speed behind an impact to get the person receiving it to move. As a result, kick shields help develop impact, agility, power and endurance, as shown via the techniques in the pictures above.

Ground Impacts

As you can see, impacts aren't exclusively kicks or punches: They can be made on small points or even on other surfaces, like the ground. In fact, many martial arts instructors recognize the importance of learning how to fall safely or how to take your opponent to the ground. Kapap practitioners just incorporate the most effective concepts from these styles into their personal defense systems. The following sequences show how versatile and flexible ground impacts can be.

EXAMPLE 1: Rocking Chair

Whether you are armed, unarmed, whether you fall voluntarily or involuntarily, this is the proper way to fall, as taught by the Kapap Academy. It is taken from traditional Japanese styles, in which the art of falling is known as *ukemi*. To fall backward, Tad Nelson controls his descent so he doesn't end up sprawled on the floor (1-3). By falling on the largest area of impact, his back, Nelson won't hurt himself. If he falls correctly, too, he'll be able to use the momentum of his fall like a rocking chair to spring back up.

EXAMPLE 2: Full Nelson Defense

In this movement, Nelson grabs Scott Seroll from behind with the intention of doing a full nelson (1). To defend himself, Seroll puts his hands on his forehead and presses (2). This prevents Nelson from controlling him with a full nelson. Next, Seroll tries to free himself by using a balance displacement—tripping Nelson (3-4). He then succeeds in bringing Nelson to the ground (5).

Chapter 6

EXAMPLE 3: Rear-Naked Choke Defense

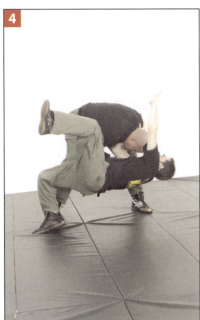
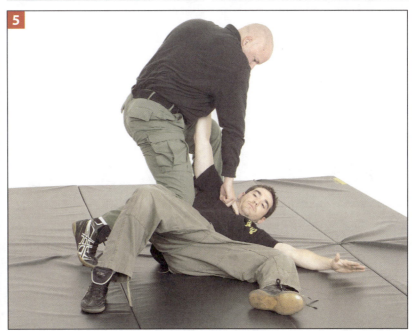

Seroll attempts a rear-naked choke against Nelson (1). Nelson uses a common wrestling move to flip Seroll and throw him to the ground (2-4). From here, Nelson can either escape or hold his opponent in place (5).

EXAMPLE 4: Rear-Body Choke Defense

There are many impacts in this scenario because Seroll uses several ways to change his relative position. When Nelson bear-hugs him to control his arms (1), Seroll elbows his attacker in the gut to get into a better relative position (2). This doesn't work, so Seroll slaps and grabs at Nelson's groin (3). When this doesn't work, he slips his right leg around Nelson's right leg, causing a balance displacement (4). Nelson hits the ground with Seroll, who is now on top of him (5). Seroll then swiftly moves to a better relative position (6).

EXAMPLE 5: Roundhouse Defense to Full Takedown

When Nelson is attacked with a right roundhouse kick, he immobilizes Seroll's leg by holding onto it (1). Because Nelson has done a lot of impact conditioning, he is able to absorb the blow to his side and immediately react with a knee to Seroll's groin (2). This causes a balance displacement, which Nelson facilitates by pushing Seroll's shoulder and pulling his leg (3-5).

Leg Impacts

Regardless of whether you are standing or lying on the ground, your legs are powerful sources of impact force. The following sequence shows you how leg impacts can help you maintain a strong relative position even if you're wounded.

OPTION 1: Ground Defense Against Kicks and Stomps

Even though Tad Nelson is on the ground, he is still able to control Avi Nardia with his legs (1). Every time Nardia approaches him, Nelson thrusts out with his foot to kick (2-3). In order to escape, Nelson could try to use his legs to unbalance his opponent (4). To make this training more reality-based, Nelson could have one leg immobilized to simulate an injury. He could also have an instructor spray water in his eyes to simulate temporary blindness, which is a real scenario that many law-enforcement and military personnel face.

Impact Combinations

Real conflicts are difficult to prepare for because you never know how they will occur, so you need a variety of impacts in your "toolbox" in order to always have enough options for any situation. In addition, don't be afraid to combine impacts from different categories because you never know which impact could save your life. When you do combinations, keep the kapap principles of movement and relative position in mind because you always want to be in the best position in a fight.

SCENARIO 1: Front Defense With the High-Low-High Triangle

In a face-to-face combat position (1), an attacker throws a straight punch at Avi Nardia's face. To maintain his distance and a stronger relative position, Nardia blocks the attack (2). This is the most economical movement for him to perform at this moment. Nardia then keeps the fluidity of his motion by stepping in past his opponent's fist with a palm strike (3). The palm strike is high while the follow-up groin strike is low (4). This confuses the attacker, allowing Nardia to keep his better relative position. He then applies a masking technique to his opponent in order to take him to the ground (5).

Scenario 2: Front Defense With Balance Displacement

In this scenario, the two opponents face each other (1). Nardia dodges a straight punch, causing his opponent to overextend and lose his balance (2). Nardia quickly steps in (3), pivots around the distracted attacker to the rear, hits low at the groin (4), and then attacks high by applying a masking technique (5).

Knife Impacts

While it isn't pleasant to imagine being attacked with a weapon, it happens a lot in our modern society, which is why this chapter also includes knife impacts. For knife training, kapap instructors teach their students how to deal with an armed attacker and how to use a knife against an attacker, if necessary. While rubber knives are used for safety, instructors prefer not to use padding during training in order to simulate the pain caused from knife cuts, which helps prepare students for a real knife fight. Because people naturally overreact when cut by a knife, they can leave themselves open to a potentially fatal mistake in a deadly situation. Remember to exercise extreme caution during knife training, which should be performed only under the supervision of a qualified instructor.

Stab and Cut Drills

Kapap's six knife-training drills show students the most effective areas to attack and how to defend against those attacks. The drills also help students improve their confidence and mobility while holding a blade, and they learn how to gauge the distance between the knife and its target.

The student who practices attacking his partner remains stationary. However, the knife should never touch the partner because a stab with a rubber knife can be painful. When performing the following drills, a student's goal is to "cut" or "stab" the following vital targets: the wrist, throat, abdomen, biceps, armpit, kidney or liver.

Drill 1: The kapap student cuts from the top left shoulder to the right side of the waist in a diagonal direction.

Drill 2: This time, the student cuts at his instructor from the top right shoulder down to the left side of the waist in a diagonal direction.

Continued on next page

KAPAP: Combat Concepts

Drill 3: The student cuts from his left to right across the opponent's abdomen.

Drill 4: This is the reverse of drill three because the student cuts from right to left across the opponent's abdomen.

Drill 5: The student stabs straight to the abdomen.

Drill 6: The student stabs straight to the throat.

Stick Drills

Kapap instructors use sticks to help students learn how to control a knife attacker and understand the power of knife impacts. In this drill, the student tries to control the instructor, who is attacking him with a stick. If he attempts to block the stick, his opponent will still be free to attack him. However, if he stops the person who holds the weapon, he controls them both.

INCORRECT OPTION 1

Avi Nardia blocks his opponent's wrist (1). Because Nardia isn't controlling the weapon, his opponent can strike Nardia's head with the weapon (2).

INCORRECT OPTION 2

Never block the top of the stick or blade because that will cause serious injury to your arm.

CORRECT OPTION

Nardia correctly defends himself from a stick impact by using his entire forearm to block its base (1). He then wraps his arm around his opponent's arm to twist the stick out of the man's grip (2-3). Nardia doesn't try to control the stick; instead, he controls his opponent's arm. Nardia can now use the stick against his opponent. It's better to control the person holding the weapon than the weapon held by the person.

Chapter 6

Knife-Defense Scenarios

The following scenarios illustrate a few ways kapap practitioners might avoid knife attacks with impacts of their own.

SCENARIO 1: Ice-Pick Attack

An attacker with an ice pick ambushes a man (1). To control the situation, the man grabs the arm holding the weapon (2). Because the man grabs the attacker's forearm rather than the ice pick, he can now wrap him into a choke hold with the ice pick pointed at the attacker's head (3-4).

KAPAP: Combat Concepts

SCENARIO 2: Knife Attack

An armed opponent attacks the defender with a knife (1). The defender blocks the cut to his wrist by grabbing the man's forearm (2) and using the kapap principle of economy of motion to trap the attacker in a wrist lock (3). While pulling the knife arm, the defender punches at the attacker's face in order to get into a strong relative position (4). He does this by slipping his arm around the opponent's trapped limb (5). Next, he takes him to the ground by walking in a circle to cause a balance displacement (6-8) and ends with a finishing maneuver and the knife in his hand (9).

Chapter 6

SCENARIO 3: Knife Fight

In the above sequence, the man on the right is armed and the other is not (1). To control the situation and the weapon, the defender steps in and puts his left arm against his opponent's shoulder (2). He uses his right hand to gain control of the opponent's knife hand and then uses his weight to pull the attacker down, causing a balance displacement (3). The unarmed man can now easily force the blade away from himself and point it at the attacker (4).

****

No matter the impact, weapon or exercise, kapap practitioners strive to practice their impact attacks and defenses in realistic training scenarios that prepare them for real conflicts. To do that effectively, always remember your relative position and ask the following questions: How do my current abilities and experiences affect my training? What techniques can I use and how strong an impact can I make with them? Once you know, then find the most qualified teachers and effective techniques from which you can upgrade your "toolbox" for any possible real-life conflict.

CHAPTER 7: LIABILITY IN THE MODERN WORLD

Power kicks, strikes, defenses and attacks are essential to martial arts and combat systems, but what most practitioners forget is that they are liable for their actions, and there are consequences. It's not a pleasant idea to dwell on, but well-balanced fighters like kapap practitioners must be aware of their responsibility to know the self-defense laws of the place they live, the area they plan to travel to, or the location where they practice their skills. Laws vary from place to place and culture to culture, which is why it is vital that a kapap practitioner seeks out resources to understand how a court of law might judge him if he needed to use his self-defense skills.

Our experience with law enforcement and the military has given us a good idea about what legal issues a person might face after defending himself. However, because criminal and civil-liability laws are constantly modified in places like the United States, it's always better to check with a legal adviser. Liability is a grave matter, whether you are a kapap practitioner or not, and there is no way to avoid it, but we hope to give you a starting point from which to work. The following chart shows what level of techniques and level of force you may legally consider using during a conflict:

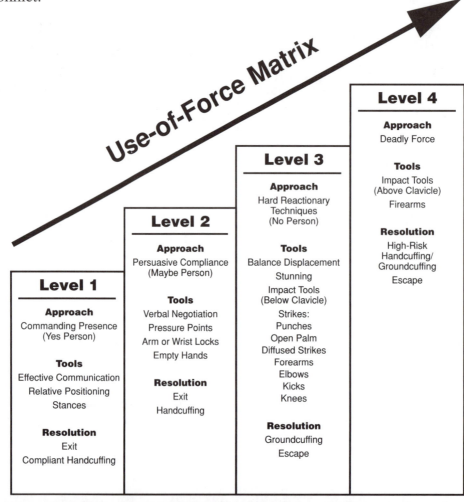

Level 1
The situations in this level involve "yes" people (See Page 20.) who are cooperative and compliant, so there is little need for you to use force. When in this situation, use mild techniques—such as strong verbal communication, body language, awareness and common sense—to control the situation.

Level 2
A level-two conflict involves a "maybe" person who might escalate the situation by turning into a "no" person, which requires a higher level of force. This is why you should always be on your guard and ready to reassess your relative position. If you decide that level-two force is necessary, use persuasion techniques like verbal negotiation, pressure points or simple pain-compliance techniques through arm and wrist locks.

Level 3
If a person physically assaults you in such a way that causes bodily injury, you are dealing with a level-three force situation and a "no" person. In this column of the matrix, you are in a situation in which you 1) can't retreat and 2) must use physical force. At this level, the law may allow you to use weapon defense, balance displacement, stunning or impact tools such as arm strikes, leg strikes or grappling.

Level 4
This deadly force level means an aggressor not only has physically assaulted you but also is going to cause you serious bodily injury or death. This is the most dangerous situation because you are certain, beyond a shadow of a doubt, that you will be seriously injured or killed. This level is regarded as "the last resort" for someone under attack. To avoid liabilities, you must be certain about the aggressor's intent and ability to grievously harm you. In a situation like this, the law may allow you to use conventional or improvised weapons, choke defenses and other deadly force techniques.

****

The use-of-force matrix is only a guideline and isn't set in stone. Each level has its own gray areas. For example, some countries allow you to use level-three force when someone attacks you with a nonlethal weapon like pepper spray; others don't. So what do you do?

When dealing with issues of liability, it's always best to be certain and research the local laws or consult a legal adviser. It's also important for students to know that they can be held liable for any force they use—even if it's done in self-defense. Remember that a well-balanced fighter studies the entire spectrum of self-defense, which includes how the law might interpret his or her defensive actions. So seek out resources on specific restrictions, regulations and procedures that are mandated by law. Also consider this chapter as a guide on how a conflict should end: You are safe and free.

ABOUT THE KAPAP ACADEMY

Formed in 2005 by Avi Nardia and Albert Timen, the Kapap Academy is located in River Edge, New Jersey, and serves as a repository of knowledge and experience where people, no matter their skill level, are "always the student and sometimes the teacher." This motto not only sets the Kapap Academy apart from other self-defense systems but also shows that it's OK for people to fail while training because you need to experience failure in order to learn and succeed.

A *kapap* instructor defines his system and not vice versa, which makes every kapap instructor's curriculum unique. Courses are customized for security companies and departments, law-enforcement agencies, military personnel and civilians who are interested in improving their self-defense skills and knowledge. The Kapap Academy believes that only through a combination of strategic learning with realistic training can professional and practical solutions be offered in modern high-stress situations.

There is no belt system, so instructors and students are typically divided into four categories:

1. **Beginner**—The student who is just beginning to understand kapap's principles.

2. **Novice**—The student who understands the moves and basic principles.

3. **Intermediate**—The student who has a working knowledge of basic patterns, tactical themes and strategies of kapap.

4. **Advanced**—The student who has practical real-life experience in applying kapap's principles and strategies and has completed the other levels.

If you're interested in becoming involved with kapap through the Kapap Academy, visit www.kapapacademy.com to find approved kapap schools and instructors in your area. If there isn't an active school or instructor nearby, you can attend a kapap seminar and use this book as a basic reference guide to kapap's concepts.

ABOUT THE AUTHORS

Maj. Avi Nardia, who is now in the Israeli Reserves, is the son of Josef Nardia, a Jewish immigrant to Palestine and member of the Israeli Special Forces. Therefore, it can be of no surprise that Josef Nardia was the first person to introduce Avi Nardia to *kapap*.

From his father, Avi Nardia learned *lochama zeira*, the military name for kapap at the time, as well as elements of judo, *jujutsu*, hand-to-hand combat, knife defense and mental endurance. At age 14, Nardia followed in his father's footsteps by joining the Israeli Military Academy as a cadet. Once there, he was exposed to many styles of combat and learned that mental readiness and a proper mind-set for conflict were paramount to preparation.

When Nardia completed his training at the academy, he joined the army. After five years, Nardia left the Israeli military in 1985 in order to study traditional martial arts and other forms of training. He went to Japan, where he spent seven years studying *kendo*, *iaido*, judo, jujutsu and *kyudo*. He also worked as a bodyguard to gain practical experience with hand-to-hand combat. When he returned to Israel in 1992, Nardia established the Israeli Kendo Federation, where he taught the martial arts he had learned. Eventually, he became involved with self-defense courses in which he taught kapap techniques to civilians at the universities of Tel Aviv and Bar Ilan. Because of these courses, the Israeli Police invited him to lead the hand-to-hand combat department of the YAMAM unit, where he continued teaching his kapap principles, and from these training sessions, kapap combat concepts were born.

Over the years, Nardia has gained experience and certification as a fencing, jujutsu, kendo, Thai boxing, fitness, rappelling, diving, boxing, *Krav Maga*, *lotar*, defensive-tactics, shooting and kapap instructor. He is also a range safety officer for the National Rifle Association and a certified coach and personal trainer. In 2000, Nardia began promoting kapap internationally through the Kapap Academy. Since then, he has taught courses on kapap, Krav Maga, lotar, tactical shooting, defensive shooting, high-risk entry, VIP protection, aircraft/bus/train interdiction, command-post procedures and intelligence gathering. He is now based in the United States, where he plays an active role in the evolution of kapap as a modern martial art and reality-based self-defense system.

KAPAP: Combat Concepts

Advanced Staff Sgt. Maj. Albert Timen has been the president of the Kapap Academy since it was officially established in 2005. At a young age, Timen studied judo and boxing before joining the Israeli military. Having grown up believing that he should serve only the best unit, Timen became part of a division that practiced lotar counterterrorism tactics. While going through the grueling lotar preparation course, known as the *Maslul*, Timen was exposed to many aspects of combat, including one-on-one and multiple-opponent scenarios.

As a former lotar and close-quarters combat instructor for various SWAT schools, Timen has been involved in hundreds of missions. He is also one of the few security operatives in the world to have subdued and arrested a "live" suicide bomber. The bomber still had his explosive belt strapped on and was caught attempting to carry out a terrorist attack. In his 18 years of operational experience, Timen has trained special units in tactics and he has cross-trained with the best operational units in the world. He is a certified Krav Maga, lotar, defensive-tactics, kapap and shooting instructor as well as a certified emergency-medical technician and range safety officer.

About the Advisers

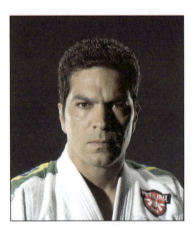

Special Adviser John Machado is a fifth-degree black belt and the nephew of Carlos Gracie, the founder of modern Brazilian *jiu-jitsu*. Recognized and respected for both his teaching expertise and his outstanding fighting and competitive accomplishments, Machado is one of the foremost jiu-jitsu authorities. His talent has been showcased in several major motion pictures and television appearances. Since he first began his training more than 20 years ago, he has won numerous awards and competitions. He has also developed his own style of Brazilian jiu-jitsu for practical use, which he has taught to the Los Angeles Police Department, the Los Angeles County Sheriff's Department and the Israeli Secret Service. For more than four years, he has worked with Avi Nardia and the Kapap Academy on developing different forms of training. For more information about John Machado, visit www.johnmachado.net.

Editorial Adviser Tad Nelson heads the Southern California Kapap Association and has been associated with the Kapap Academy since its inception. With more than 18 years of combined military and law-enforcement experience, Nelson is able to use his accumulated practical knowledge and apply it to his kapap training. Nelson is also a range safety officer for the Kapap Academy's tactical handgun course. For more information about kapap in Southern California, visit www.socalkapap.com.